Dear Aunt Sue,

May God use these words to bring you closer to Him — to give you a deep love for Jesus! And May you never forget the gospel.

Love ever, Jesus!

Emma

Gospel Amnesia

Forgetting the Goodness of the News

Luma Simms

GCD Books is the publishing branch of Gospel Centered Discipleship.com. GCD exists to promote discipleship resources that help make, mature, and multiply disciples of Jesus.

Copyright ©2013 by Luma Simms

ISBN: 978-1494841171

All rights reserved. No part of this publication may be reproduced in any form without written permission from the author. Made and designed in the United States of America.

Cover design by Josh Shank of RocketRepublic.com

The clarity with which Luma articulates the gospel of grace is given force by the honesty with which she brings it to bear on her own life, past and present. The result is a refreshing book I enjoyed reading and am happy to commend warmly to others."
—**Dane Ortlund, Senior Vice President, Crossway**

"Luma Simms remembers vividly what it was like to be simply going through the motions of a spiritual life. She writes like someone who has just been awakened from a nightmare and can still describe it in detail. Luma's voice communicates the pain of forgetting what matters most, and may be just the voice to reach the half-awake."
—**Fred Sanders, Associate Professor of Theology, Torrey Honors Institute, Biola University**

"*Gospel Amnesia* culls piercing insights from some of the best gospel authors, while also healing the wounds with explanatory words of grace. In bold honesty, Luma Simms puts the liberating power of the gospel on display. This book is for anyone who wants grace to pulse stronger in their lives."
—**Jonathan Dodson, Author of** *Gospel-Centered Discipleship, Raised? Finding Jesus by Doubting the Resurrection* (Feb, 2014) and *The Unbelievable Gospel: Say Something Worth Believing* (September, 2014)

"The message in *Gospel Amnesia* is loud and clear: Jesus loves you. This book is theologically rich and punctuated by Luma's personal accounts of her own "gospel amnesia"—a forgetting of the gospel that many of us can relate to. In *Gospel Amnesia*, you'll be reminded afresh of your First Love and be awestruck again by the wonders of his love."
—**Gloria Furman**, **Author of** *Glimpses of Grace*

"Reading *Gospel Amnesia* will cause you to wake up and have your eyes opened to where you have forgotten the gospel. It will leave you rejoicing in God's love in the gospel, committed to beholding that love, and keeping it in focus for the rest of life."
—**Keri Folmar, Author,** *Joy! A Bible Study on Philippians for Women*

"The gospel isn't meant to be a means for justification and then forgotten. Luma Simms has a diagnosis. Anytime we reduce the gospel and dismiss it or attempt to move away from it, we are suffering from gospel amnesia. Luma explains how this amnesia goes beyond individuals to affect relationships in local churches, missions, denominations, and even culture. Gospel Amnesia will inspire, challenge, and provoke you to see and savor Jesus Christ."
—**Trillia Newbell**, **Author of** *United: Captured by God's Vision for Diversity* **(Moody Publishers, March 2014)**

"Luma transparently opens up her journey for us, of realizing the value of the gospel, and it is so refreshing! A.W. Tozer said, "What comes to your mind when you think about God is the most important thing about you..." because your view of God defines so much of your life and how you act. Luma convictingly and effectively shows us the glory and goodness of God in the gospel for the transformation of our life. My heart is stirred."
—**Matt Brown, Founder, Think Eternity, evangelist, and author**

"With clarity and humility, Luma shows that we minimize the gospel if we relegate it to the basics of the Christian faith. *Gospel Amnesia* emphasizes the richness and centrality of the gospel—a gospel that we grow in to, rather than out of. Luma's writing reinvigorates our passion for sharing the good news with others, while also highlighting the transforming power that comes from preaching the gospel daily to ourselves."
—**Erika Allen, Editor, Crossway**

"*Gospel Amnesia* is a well-timed wake up call for our hearts. In many ways, Luma Simms reminds us of the greatest love story that we seem to have forgotten."
—**Caesar Kalinowski, Director, The GCM Collective**

"Through *Gospel Amnesia* I have been exposed, rebuked, and challenged regarding the many ways I forget, assume, and presume the gospel—rather than living out all that the gospel offers in Christ. I've also been encouraged afresh to rehearse the gospel to myself daily, as a way to keep my heart and mind joyfully focused on the person and work of Christ—not on any other object or circumstance that vies for His place in my heart. This book did some heart work that my soul needed. I pray that it does the same for all who read."
—Kristie Anyabwile, Servant of Christ; wife of Thabiti Anyabwile, First Baptist Church of Grand Cayman

"There are many recent books that lay out the theology of gospel-centered living, but *Gospel Amnesia* is a unique and practical approach. Luma Simms first brings a powerful narrative of her personal journey with an authenticity that will provoke your heart to embrace the love of Christ. She then powerfully challenges us to apply that biblical vision to how we do church, missions, and cultural engagement. The Gospel changes everything…"

—Bill Walsh, Director of International Outreach, The Gospel Coalition

To Issam and Awatif Fattohy, my parents.

Table of Contents

Acknowledgements	2
Foreword	6
Preface	9
Chapter 1: Borderline Blasphemy	12
Chapter 2: Individual Gospel Amnesia	26
Chapter 3: Gospel Amnesia and the Local Church	54
Chapter 4: Missional Gospel Amnesia	68
Chapter 5: Denominational Gospel Amnesia	78
Chapter 6: Cultural Gospel Amnesia	92
Chapter 7: Overcoming Gospel Amnesia	108
Further Reading	120

Acknowledgements

A worthwhile work is never done alone—can never be done alone. Our God has created and called his Body to work together and for his glory. As such, I have many people to thank.

Geoff, you are my best friend. I am always in danger of idolizing you, my love. Kids, you are my joy, a most precious gift from the Lord. Thank you, Mom and Dad for years of sacrifice and faithful parenting. Thank you for your support and encouragement. Thank you, Suzan, for all the years you lived through my hypocrisy. I love you. Thank you to all the family in America and Australia for your love and encouragement.

Thank you to my editor, Ben Roberts, for believing in *Gospel Amnesia*. And to GCD president Jonathan Dodson and directors Brad Watson and Brandon Smith for their continued support. Thank you to all the GCD Press staff for your work and support on this project. Josh, I don't know how to thank you for your cover design. You took my ideas and vision and brought it to life in powerful and beautiful art. It was as though this was exactly what *Gospel Amnesia* was supposed to look like. Thank you!

Thank you to our friend Andy Fletcher, on whose blog I first read the words "gospel amnesia." Thank you Andy and Kendra for telling others about waking up to the gospel, and for not being afraid to talk about hard things.

Thank you Megan Lindsay for listening to the manuscript and giving feedback and suggestions. Thank you for theological conversations that sharpened me. Thank you for praying for me faithfully for years for the Lord to release me from the bondage of gospel amnesia and to revive my soul. The Lord answered your prayers! Thank you for wrestling with God, like Jacob, for loving and desiring Jesus, even when you didn't understand. You have taught me a lot about what it means to have a real friendship through the thin and thick of life. "Faithful are the wounds of a friend" (Proverbs 27:6).

Thank you to my faithful friend, Gloria Furman. Your consistent encouragement, your gospel–loving heart, your missionary service in Dubai, your belief in what I was trying to do with *Gospel Amnesia*, long phone conversations, theological sharpening, and your Sibbes quotes have been a blessing and a gift from the Lord. I think I would have given up if it had not been for the Lord encouraging me through you.

Thank you Keri Folmar for being a prayer warrior for me and this book. You have been a mentor and a faithful friend. Thank you for encouraging me in my writing and for your love and knowledge of God's Word. Thank you for your desire and work to help women love the Word of God. And thank you for your missionary service in Dubai. You have been such an example to me, Keri.

Thank you Pastor Brian Bowman for listening to me read the manuscript and giving feedback and suggestions. Thank you for your support and

and encouragement of my writing and for reminding me that I need Jesus, again and again. We're blessed to have you as our Pastor.

Thank you to Cathi and Randy Kutz for believing in *Gospel Amnesia* when it was still just a small seed in my mind. Thank you for the hospitality in your home and the week we spent talking about gospel amnesia, Jesus, and what God was working out in our hearts. Randy, thank you for telling me you would buy the book for the title alone. I will never forget that, it carried me through many bumps. Your visionary and missionary hearts have been such an encouragement!

We are grateful for our community group at Valley Life Church. Your faithful prayers while I was writing were very much appreciated. Thank you, Joy, for checking in on me.

Thank you to all the following people who prayed for me and this project and who encouraged me while I was writing: Wendy Alsup, Kim Ballam, Leslie Ducharme, Kristina Gallarzo (who walked the road of gospel amnesia in similar ways right along with me), JoAnne Markov, Tonya McHale, Mike and Stacey Munoz, Heather Neufeld, and Nancy and David Saar.

I am grateful to Pastor Randy Booth who shepherded me during a hard season. Thank you to elders Richard Klaus, Dirk Uphoff and Rob Withem, for preaching the gospel during the time the Lord was reviving my heart. Thank you to pastor, Jeff Niell, who taught me about grace when my heart was very far from it.

Foreword

Oh, this is a good book. So good. It's good like a doctor is good who accurately diagnoses your disease and prescribes an effective treatment. The illness isn't good and you could wish that you didn't have it. But you do, and when you're sick what you really need is a good physician (Luke 5:31).

I have had this sickness of gospel amnesia. And I still suffer at times this "defect in memory... resulting from pathological cause"[1]—my pathologically selfish sin nature. I can forget the gospel in all sorts of ways—in as many ways as I can be proud. Countless.

My pathetic pride! It can block my memory and blind my spiritual eyes causing me to forget that apart from Jesus I am nothing and can do nothing (John 15:5). How easily I can focus on busy *doings* and forget about *trusting*. How quickly I can lose sight of Jesus's glory and desire my own. It is disturbing how easily God's grace toward me dulls in my affections while my longing surges strong to be someone worthy of praise, whose efforts win God's acceptance or the world's.

Gospel Amnesia can be so severe that I have talked about the gospel and forgot it at the same time, because I was thinking mainly about impressing others not imparting grace to them. Pitiful. And if untreated, it can

---

[1] "Amnesia." *The Free Dictionary*. Farlex, n.d. Web. 30 Nov. 2013. <http://www.thefreedictionary.com/amnesia>.

be deadly.

If you're a Christian, the sobering truth is that you succumb to this sickness too.

That's why I think this book is so important and why I'm thrilled for you to read it! It's a remedy of remembering for gospel forgetfulness. And Luma Simms is such a wonderful soul-physician. This is no cold clinical analysis. Luma writes passionately as one who knows this disease from the inside. With a beautiful, transparent, and at times raw humility she makes herself Exhibit A of Gospel Amnesia. As she describes her experiences you will recognize yours and the grace she has discovered will fuel your faith for transformation.

Luma says it like it is and, if you're like me, sometimes that will sting. That's okay. "Faithful are the wounds of a friend" (Proverbs 27:6), especially if that friend has suffered from the same malady afflicting you. There is nothing like straight talk that is laced with the compassion and empathy that only comes from having struggled in the same ways.

What you hold in your hands is, I believe, a Godsend. It is grace. It will help you recognize the symptoms of Gospel Amnesia, alert you to its dangers, and give you very practical help in overcoming it. It will do all this by pointing you directly to Jesus and help you remember what is of "first importance" (1 Corinthians 15:3).

I join Luma in the hopes that this book will "encourage

you to look at the cross [and] fall in love with Jesus anew or maybe for the first time." Read, remember, and be healed.

Jon Bloom

President, Desiring God

Preface

I used to be a Christian who did not think about Jesus. I used to be a Christian who was bored with Jesus. I remember telling my husband one day that I was tired of him telling me "Jesus loves you, Luma." It all seemed trite and superficial. I wanted, I needed, something deeper. Something more challenging to my mind, more impactful than "Jesus died on the cross for your sins." That tired story, heard countless times since my father first spoke the gospel to me in a train station in Thessaloniki, rang hollow. Despite my weakness, ambivalence, and even hostility, this same gospel has never let me go, will not let me go—through hardships, divorce, rebellion, passivity, legalism, and back again. Although I believe I have been a Christian since I was eight years old, for many years it was with a cloudiness and distortion like that of the blind man Jesus healed in Mark 8:24 "... I see men, but they look like trees walking." It hurts to write these words, yet they must be written. They must be written for the sake of many who silently live the way I lived and think the way I thought.

Most of my life has been spent finding one way or another to atone for myself. Operating from a hazy understanding of what Christ did in his life and death to gain my salvation, this self-atonement was like a vortex, a downward spiral into the depth of my amnesia. I wanted to be "godly," and I thought I had a pretty good idea of how to go about it. However, the harder I tried to approximate the image in my head of what a godly woman was supposed to be, the worse my depression, panic attacks, and rage became. I poisoned our household with my anger and "holy" laws. Down I went like a dragon falling from the sky with blood and fire spilling everywhere and contaminating everything in its path. At the end of hope, feeling and believing myself to be on the receiving end of the hot displeasure and disappointment of a Holy God, I crashed. And then, when there was nothing left of me, there was Jesus. Savior, Redeemer, Friend. No displeasure, no disappointment, just the blazing fire of unmerited grace.

Chastened by the wonder of his glory, I am now able to tell you about a Savior who was not ashamed to condescend to love and save a woman like me. A woman at his feet—a woman of the cross. The ultimate goal of *Gospel Amnesia* is nothing short of the following exhortation: I know your deeds; you have the reputation of being alive, but you are dead. Wake up! (Revelation 3:1b-2a)

Dietrich Bonhoeffer said, "When Christ calls a man, he bids him come and die." I invite you to the same; come, and die, and be raised again to live to Christ.

Some of us have forgotten the love we had at first. (Rev. 2:4) Others of us are like lukewarm water, neither hot nor cold, good only for spitting out (Rev. 3:15–17). Whoever we are, and wherever our amnesic tendencies lie, we need the white hot fire of the gospel—now, today (Hebrews 3:12–15).

CHAPTER ONE:

Borderline Blasphemy

I remember a time as a dedicated Christian desiring to do good works and be pleasing to God, when I found myself thinking: "If I hear the name of Jesus one more time I'm going to scream, if I hear the word 'missional' one more time I'm going to be sick, if I hear the word 'gospel' and how loving and gracious Jesus is... I'm going to..." I didn't think much of it at the time. I thought it was a problem with other people and how they "did church."

When the Holy Spirit brought it to my memory a year later, it took my breath away. The eyes of my heart were opened and I saw those statements for what they really were: The edge of blasphemy. "How did I get here?" I wondered. How did I ever get to a place where I could be sick of hearing the name of my Lord and Savior? How did I get to the point where I would actually *say* to myself that I was sick and tired of hearing about the gospel, that I needed and wanted to "move on" from it?

After a year in which the blindness was removed one hard crusty piece at a time, all my thoughts finally coalesced when I found these words from D.A. Carson:

> Recognize that students do not learn everything you teach them. They certainly do not learn everything I

teach them! What *do* they learn? They learn what I am excited about; they learn what I emphasize, what I return to again and again; they learn what organizes the rest of my thought. So if I happily *presuppose* the gospel but rarely articulate it and am never excited about it, while effervescing frequently about, say, ecclesiology or textual criticism, my students may conclude that the most important thing to me is ecclesiology or textual criticism. They may pick up my *assumption* of the gospel; alternatively, they may even distance themselves from the gospel; but what they will almost certainly do is place at the center of *their* thought ecclesiology or textual criticism, thereby wittingly or unwittingly marginalizing the gospel... Part of my obligation as a scholar–teacher, a scholar–pastor is... never to lose my passion for living and thinking and being excited about what must remain at the center. Failure in this matter means I lead my students and parishioners astray... I must be concerned for what I am passing on to the next generation. Its configuration, its balance and focus. I dare never forget that students do not learn everything I try to teach them but primarily what I am excited about.[2]

You see, my heart used to be a very sick heart. I was a Christian, but I fancied that I had progressed past the gospel, seeing it as something that was only for the

---

[2] Andrew David Naselli, "*D.A. Carson's Theological Method*," Scottish Bulletin of Evangelical Theology (2011): 248–249 (Emphases in the original)

unsaved, only for becoming a Christian. I set my heart on other things at the expense of cherishing Christ. What I was excited about was becoming a "godly" wife and woman, being content in domesticity and doing it well, offering unparalleled hospitality, keeping my children as far away from worldliness as possible, homeschooling because it was the only truly "godly" way of educating children, healthy whole food eating because that meant I was in line with a more "biblically agrarian" type of living, singing only Psalms and hymns in worship because that was "more honoring," and on and on... you get the picture. So, I had in some sense presupposed the gospel, and not always "happily," as in Carson's hypothetical. This presupposition turned into presumption, and then full-scale forgetfulness and blindness.

I had "gospel amnesia," *big time*.

Don't let my examples sidetrack you. This book is not a denouncement of homeschooling, or a diatribe against Psalms and hymns, or condemnation of a healthy diet, or a renouncement of any good thing that ensnared my heart. Satan would love to distract you with a red herring. *This book is about the affliction of assuming, forgetting, and marginalizing the gospel; the symptoms of this condition, and its one cure.*

If we presuppose the gospel, like I did (like many do), rarely articulate its profundity and are never excited about it while "effervescing frequently" about—pick what excites you—then for all intents and purposes we have gospel amnesia. We have lived in such a way as to "tell" those around us, and the world, that the gospel is to be assumed, presumed, and subsumed while our "Christian" life orbits some other center (Illustration 1, below).

Illustration 1: Gospel amnesia by marginalizing Christ

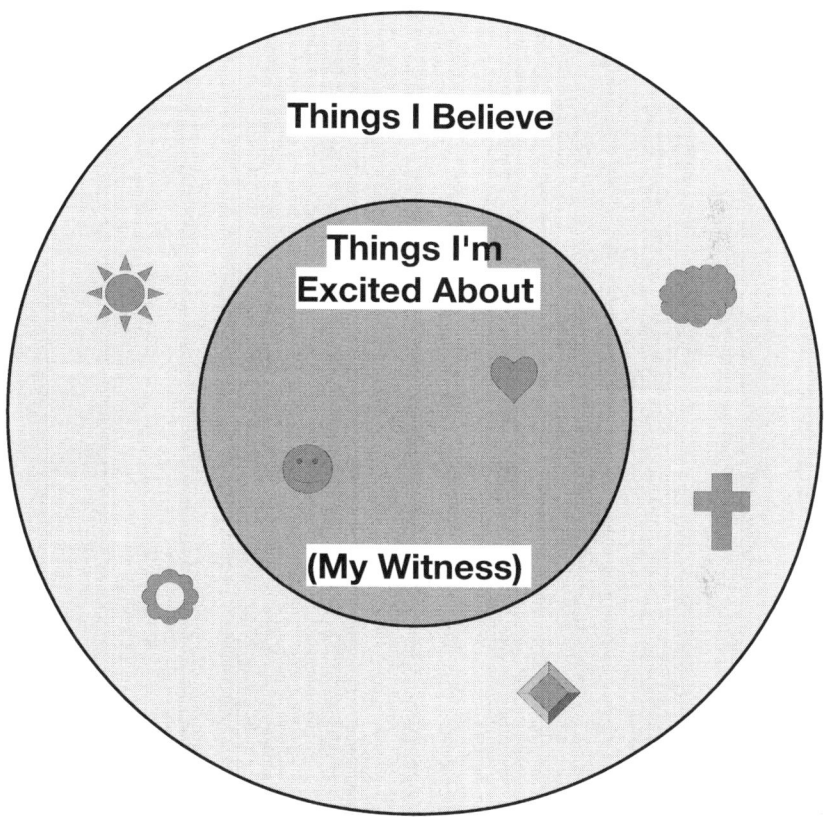

What makes gospel amnesia particularly pernicious is the belief that we are "doing right" because what is exciting us, in many cases, is a "good thing." We all know that there are many ways to sin. However, if we are every day embracing the gospel, washing our eyes out with it, there is quick and abundant grace and forgiveness through Christ when we find ourselves in sin. When we have gospel amnesia, our mind may be occupied with other things, good and necessary things, even Christianly things, and because these have subtly *displaced* the gospel and it has become dim and distant, we lose sight of that clear and quick path back to abundant grace. There is an extra barrier in the way, the barrier of our Christian idols—"clean" idols—and our own pride about being a "good Christian." The Bible calls this sin *blindness*. But Christ died for this sin too. His grace has already conquered it.

Let us return to his abundant grace.

WHAT IS THE GOSPEL

In the grace of God, today we have many outstanding books that articulate the gospel in fresh and compelling ways, and I have tried to list several in the recommended reading list at the end of the book. For the purpose of this book, it will be helpful to state a working definition of the gospel before going further:

Jesus Christ, the only begotten son of God, who existed in communion with the Father before anything came into being, took on human flesh and became a man so as to be the savior of men, who are all hopelessly sinful in themselves, and to be the mediator between holy God and sinful man. In the incarnation he was born of a virgin, lived a perfect and sinless life, obeying and fulfilling the law God had given to his covenant people,

Israel. He died by being crucified, his body nailed to the cross, taking on the full wrath of God against sin. On the third day he rose again through the power of God. He has ascended to the right hand of the Father where he rules over all. One day he will return to judge and to transform all creation (Illustration 2, below).

Illustration 2: Christ and the gospel at the center

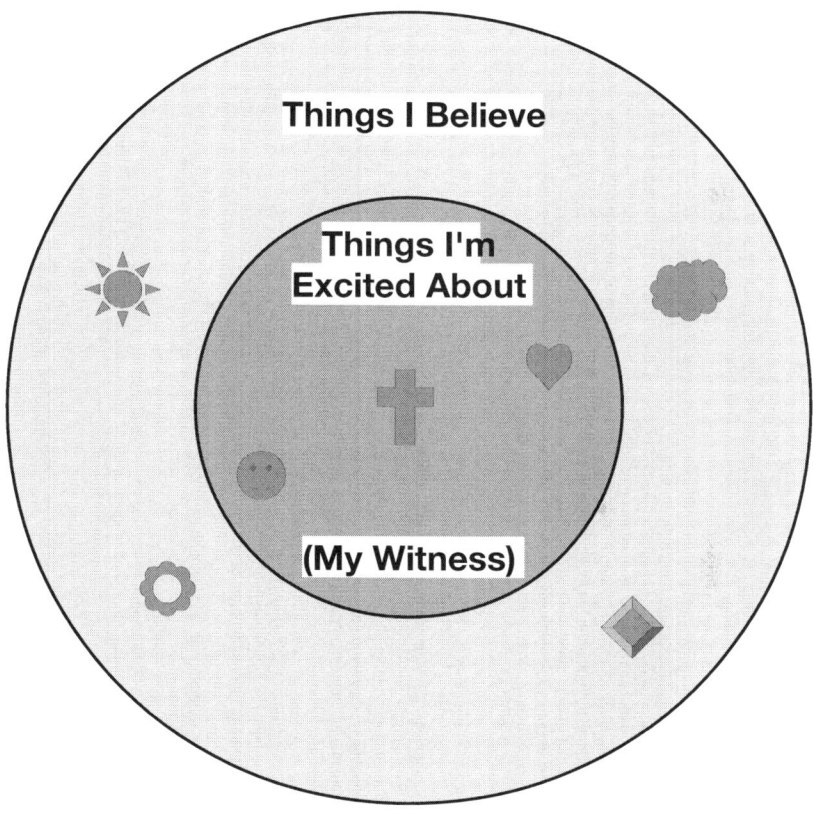

Tim Keller has said, "The gospel has been described as a pool in which a toddler can wade and yet an elephant can swim. It is both simple enough to tell to a child and profound enough for the greatest minds to explore.

Indeed, even angels never tire of looking into it (1 Peter 1:12)."[3]

If angels never tire of it, what is our excuse?

WHAT IS GOSPEL AMNESIA

Amnesia means a partial or complete loss of memory. Although it is said that every time we sin that is a time when we forget the gospel, here I am talking about an extensive degradation or suppression of our consciousness of the gospel.

What I am calling "gospel amnesia," is a condition which takes on several forms that interfere with or diminish our **reliance** on the person and work of Jesus Christ (Illustration 3, below):

In form one, I call it the **Distraction Mode**; we Christians get so caught up in the doing that we forget to be believing; we functionally abandon the gospel. There is very little or no dwelling on the person and cross work of Christ. Affection for Jesus is slight or non-existent. This form may be summed up well in the words of Screwtape, "We thus distract men's minds from Who He is, and what He did."[4] This is essentially the gospel: Who He is and what He did. Gospel amnesia is a powerful tool in the hands of our Enemy. It's important to mention that we can also be distracted by

---

[3] Timothy Keller, "The Gospel in All its Forms," *Christianity Today/Leadership Journal*, Spring 2008, Volume XXIX, No. 2, 15

[4] C.S. Lewis, *The Screwtape Letter* (New York: Macmillan Publishing Company, 1982), 107

the things of the world. Hence, the **Distraction Mode** can be used to describe either being preoccupied with Christianly things or drawn away by worldly things, sometimes pursuits as good or necessary as education, career, family, and friendship.

In form two, the **Progression Mode**, some of us Christians convince ourselves that the gospel is the "basics," the "foundation," and that in order to progress in sanctification we need to move on from these basics. We think that dwelling on the gospel and rehearsing it means stagnation and a lack of spiritual maturity. In this case, I would say the gospel has become a limited set of propositions that are for "tipping us into the kingdom"[5] and no more.

Form three, the **Presumption Mode**, is when a Christian is living no different than the world. The gospel has not penetrated into the heart and transformed the mind. They presume upon the gospel and grace of God and continue to live a life for "self" instead of the Lord Jesus. As an aside, this type of Christian may also live a double life where they are "Christian" at church, with family, and around other believers but on the job or at school they have a different personality. There is always the question of whether someone like this is actually a believer. I am assuming here that this is someone who as far as we know, confesses that Jesus Christ is the Son of God, crucified, risen and will return.

---

[5] D.A. Carson

Illustration 3: Three forms of gospel amnesia, contrasted with gospel reliance

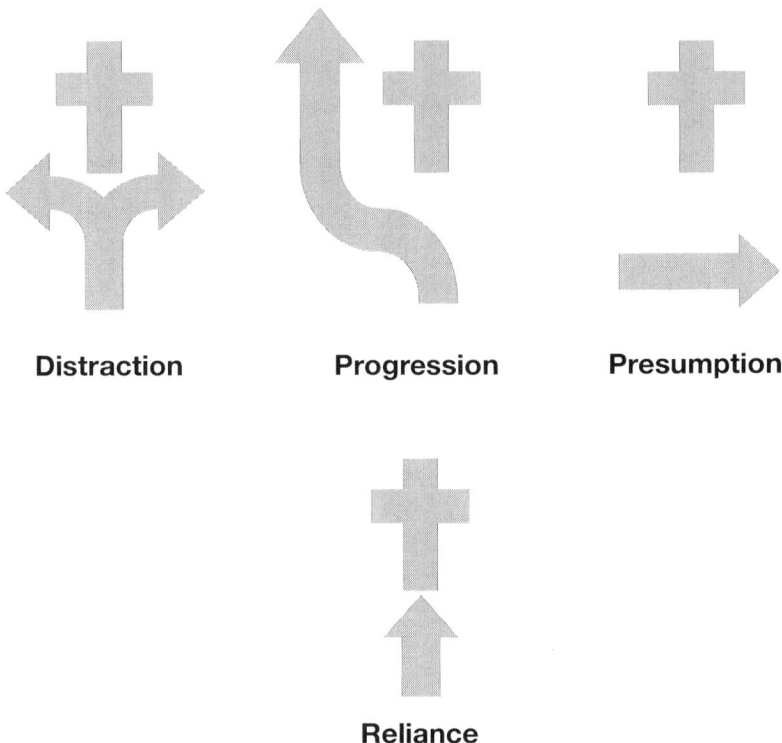

Many people may not feel they fall under any of these categories. If that is genuinely the case, then I praise God for it! Please stand firm and help the rest of us. However, I believe one of the traps we fall into, is thinking that because we intellectually understand a concept (e.g. the gospel, the atonement, hell, ecclesiology, etc.), because we've categorized and systematized our knowledge, then it means we have internalized it and are living it out. This is a form of intellectual blindness which goes hand in glove with gospel amnesia. Knowledge has no transformative power. Multitudes of Christians are "always learning and never able to arrive at a knowledge of the truth" (2 Tim. 3:7). We "have the appearance of godliness, but deny its power" (2 Tim. 3:5) because our outward behavior or understanding is not rooted in the gospel but in another center.

This is why I believe that **lukewarmness** might be an approximate synonym for gospel amnesia. I have found lukewarmness to be most deceptive and dangerous. Justin Taylor has written: "May God keep us from benign admiration of Jesus rather than true love and adoration for our Lord and Savior Jesus Christ."[6] When we combine intellectual hubris with dampened affections it results in a "benign admiration" that is *complacent at the heart level,* even if it is outwardly active. Rarely can we hope to convince such a person of the impoverishment of their heart; either they will point to their ministry/activity or hide behind doctrinally correct statements. Gospel amnesia is a blindness that only the Holy Spirit can convict and only the grace of God can heal. When you've forgotten the gospel, it's hard to see that you've forgotten the gospel *because* you have forgotten the gospel. Beloved, "whenever our heart condemns us, God is greater than our heart, and he knows everything" (1 John 3:20). When and if we are convicted in this area, we can be assured that there is abundant forgiveness with God because of Jesus.

---

[6] Justin Taylor, March 16, 2012, *"Admiration of Jesus Without Love for Jesus," Between Two Worlds,* http://thegospelcoalition.org/blogs/justintaylor/2012/03/16/admiration-of-jesus-without-love-for-jesus/ [accessed between 16 March 2012 to 7 November 2012]

In any of these cases, the Christian is not living self-consciously and deliberately within the horizon of the gospel, even *if* the person is living "Christianly" in their behavior. Christ and the cross have been forgotten, assumed, or marginalized. Eventually, in many of these cases the gospel amnesia could lead to revulsion to, or aversion from the gospel.

What is needed is gospel-aware habits trained by constant use. The writer of Hebrews says:

> About this we have much to say, and it is hard to explain, since you have become dull of hearing. For though by this time you ought to be teachers, you need someone to teach you again the basic principles of the oracles of God. You need milk, not solid food, for everyone who lives on milk is unskilled in the word of righteousness, since he is a child. But solid food is for the mature, *for those who have their powers of discernment trained by constant practice to distinguish good from evil.* — Hebrews 5:11–14 (Emphasis mine)

For many years I assumed this passage and the one following in chapter six meant that the gospel was the "milk" and that something else was the "solid food." I will say more about that error in the next chapter, but I bring these verses up now to concentrate on the last portion of verse 14. Dwelling continuously within the horizon of the gospel trains our habits. This constant practice of preaching the gospel to ourselves *every day* trains our souls to distinguish between good and evil.

Here is some wisdom from Matthew Henry to help flesh this out for pastor and sheep alike:

> It is the wisdom of ministers rightly to divide the word of truth, and to give to every one his portion—milk to babes, and strong meat to those of full age. There are spiritual senses as well as those that are natural. There is a spiritual eye, a spiritual appetite, a spiritual taste; the soul has its sensations as well as the body... *It is by use and exercise that these senses are improved, made more quick and strong to taste the sweetness of what is good and true, and the bitterness of what is false and evil. Not only reason and faith, but spiritual sense, will teach men to distinguish between what is pleasing and what is provoking to God, between what is helpful and what is hurtful to our own souls.*[7] (Emphases mine)

We see that our soul needs to be trained by the gospel daily by the exercise of our *spiritual senses*. This will be an ongoing struggle in this life, and it is central to the spiritual fight against gospel amnesia.

I have lived through all the above cases during different seasons in my 35 year walk with the Lord. I want to warn of a danger: Some might read this, and file it away as another "okay, got that." I ask that instead of reading this book merely with the power of your mind, you read this book pleading with the Holy Spirit for spiritual eyes

---

[7] Matthew Henry, *Matthew Henry's Commentary on the Whole Bible Complete and Unabridged* (Hendrickson Publishers, LLC, 1991), 2388

to see the glory of Jesus, to see the uniqueness of your own gospel amnesia.

QUESTIONS

Do you think it's possible that you have forgotten the gospel?

Do you ever get distracted by the things of the world into living as if you've forgotten the gospel?

Do you ever get distracted by "good" things (e.g. ministry, raising children, career etc.) such that you have functionally set aside the gospel?

Do you ever think that the gospel is just the basics of the Christian faith and that you have, or ought to have, progressed beyond it?

Do you ever presume upon the gospel, excusing yourself of sin or worldliness because you think it's all easily forgiven?

PRAYER

Holy Father, open my eyes. Pierce my heart. Move in my soul. Shake me out of my lukewarmness. Show me all the ways in which I have forgotten about my savior and redeemer Jesus Christ. Give me joy at his name!

Give me an insatiable desire for him. Lift up my face to behold you. Amen.

CHAPTER TWO:

Individual Gospel Amnesia

Using the truths in Carson's quote from the previous chapter, a question I am asking often in this book is: What has become the center? This question is crucial. When and if we can identify the center of our lives we can test whether or not we have marginalized Christ. I believe that it's obvious why this is an important discipline for a Christian to do periodically—this examination of the fulcrum. Without staying centered on the gospel, we stray.

What has become the center of your individual life?

When I quit law school to become an at-home-mom I swung hard and fast from an egalitarian worldview to a patriarchal model that was heavily obligation-driven and light on the gospel. (These types of over-corrections happen to many of us.) I sought maturity and order, feared grace, and looked down on the gospel because I thought it elementary. I wanted to move on (Progression Mode) from the "basics." Trying to make up for my earlier weaknesses and sins, I devoured books that told me what to *do* to become a "godly" wife and mother, how to homeschool according to ancient and classical ways, how to submit to my husband in my dress and behavior, how to keep my kids away from the world, and how to be vigilant about the world that had crept into the church. I even began grinding my own wheat berries for homemade wheat bread. I saw all these "good works" *as the way to grow in Christian maturity* and therefore, be more sanctified. Just to be clear, there is nothing wrong with reading "topical" or "method" books, *per se,* as long as in our minds these types of "help" books do not crowd out the Holy Spirit or Scripture. Furthermore, you do not have to have a list as extreme and strange as mine to have gospel amnesia.

Throughout all that time, if I were given some kind of theology test, I would certainly have answered that we enter the kingdom of God because we are justified by faith alone, through grace alone by the finished work of Christ alone. However, at some unspoken level, partly out of fear of losing God's favor, I embraced the idea that we *stayed in* by our good works. This is a very important distinction: It was not your classic "works-righteousness" where I thought I could be saved *by* my works. I believed that I was saved by God's predetermined act through grace by faith in Jesus, but that this only brought me to the state of: *Not guilty.* The *theological error* was thinking that now we *stay in* or now we *gain merit* through demonstrations of progressive sanctification. Moreover, if we are not progressing in sanctification, then maybe we will fall into apostasy. The goal was to become "more biblical" or "godly" with the meaning of the phrase being determined by certain moral and life practices. At the cost of being too simplistic it went something like this:

> Good works ⇒ progress in sanctification ⇒ verifiable justification ⇒ merit to stay in God's kingdom

And so I threw myself into all sorts of good works/biblical life choices, which in retrospect I see as fearing the work of God's grace in our lives. Reacting to the antinomianism of the surrounding culture, grace became a synonym for antinomianism in my understanding. Unfortunately, because I was not immersed in the gospel, I had a misunderstanding of true biblical grace. All I could envision was what Dietrich Bonhoeffer called "cheap grace." In *The Cost of Discipleship*, Bonhoeffer says, "Cheap grace is the deadly enemy of our Church. We are fighting today for costly grace"[8] Fighting for "costly grace" while operating outside of gospel principles, I bounded grace in such a way that I functionally gutted the grace of Christ out of the atonement.

Since the Bible says that we are recognizable as being regenerate by our works, our sinful hearts can take a short-cut of going straight to works as a demonstrable example of our justification. Often, out of fear of apostasy. Our faith in Jesus *should* give us faith to trust that he will keep his word and preserve us. It *should* give us faith that the Spirit will bear fruit in us. But I flipped the logic. Works done in the here and now mislead us into a false security. Focusing on these

---

[8] Dietrich Bonhoeffer *The Cost of Discipleship* (New York: Touchstone Simon & Schuster, 1995) 43

works was a powerful theme in my own bout of gospel amnesia, and this went on for quite a few years.

In his grace, the Lord shook me out of my blindness. We had elevated all these life prescriptions to such a degree that we were not capable of being good neighbors to our fellow believers *or* unbelievers. I struggled mightily with anger and bitterness. This came to a climax a few summers ago. Our family was suffering deeply from a year's worth of one hardship after another, some of them of our own making, some of them handed to us in the providence of God. My anger turned to rage, my bitterness became poison to everything and everyone around me. Early in the fall, in my Scripture reading I came to 1 John 2:9–11:

> Whoever says he is in the light and hates his brother is still in darkness. Whoever loves his brother abides in the light, and in him there is no cause for stumbling. But whoever hates his brother is in the darkness and walks in the darkness, and does not know where[1] he is going, because the darkness has blinded his eyes.

I was undone. I had been calling these things Christian, and yet the attitude in which I held them was anathema to Christ. At that moment I stood at the edge of a chasm, clinging to my wretchedness. I knew that if I chose the way of anger, bitterness, and rage I would be swallowed up by these sins that had dominated my life. I could feel the Holy Spirit beside me. It was clear, there was no reconciliation between the darkness of my sin and the presence of Christ. I ached for Jesus, but I loved my sins. Human words fail here, but the Holy Spirit within me chose Christ, and he loosed the shackles and broke the bondage to these sins.

Looking back now I see that the movement by the Spirit started way before that time, a few years back, while I was reading *The Prodigal God* by Tim Keller. But I fought it. I fought it because it revealed to me that I had swung from being the wandering younger brother to the self-righteous pharisaical older brother. I couldn't handle that knowledge. The story of the prodigal son in Luke 15, is the story of my life, twice over. I had invested much time and energy convincing myself that I had made up for all those years as the younger brother. It would have been soul shattering for me to have to admit that I had metamorphosed into the self-righteous older brother. In the end, as it turned out a good year and a half later, it was indeed soul tearing when the Spirit took away the last shreds of self-deception. My self-righteousness had ravaged my soul and left me desolate—nowhere to turn but to my perfectly righteous Elder Brother.

Those years were some of the most brutal for me spiritually as I fought with God while he destroyed my idols one after another.

IDOLATRY: A ROOT AND A SYMPTOM OF GOSPEL AMNESIA

One of my idols used to be the godliness and good behavior of my children in and out of the home. To be honest, I was obsessed with "godly behavior," both mine and my children's. I remember when one of our children disobeyed in front of another family, I got angry because my child had embarrassed me. I equated a young child's struggle with self control as a lack of "godliness." I worried that the other family would think we were not as "sanctified" as they were. My child's behavior had become an idol, a demigod to the idol of my own pride. If it hadn't been, I would not have been so angry and anxious. Idols do this; they are exacting, requiring we sacrifice all to them and eliciting rage from us when they are threatened. I had been elevating a faux sanctification over and above parenting my child with grace, humility and longsuffering—the way my heavenly Father parents me.

As an aside, a singular obsession with obedience to God does not necessarily equal a high view of God. It could very well equal a high view of myself. The obsession, the time and effort, all revolves around me and how I'm doing—for all the talk on "obedience" the focus is still me instead of Christ. And here is where we see the heart idolatry. The Holy Spirit lays it bare and visible to our eyes.

Gospel amnesia ushers in idolatry and vice versa. It is imperative that we discern, expose and destroy[9] the set of idols that tempt us within our Christian subculture. In his sermon, *The Grand Demythologizer*, Pastor Timothy Keller uses the text from Acts 19:23–41 to

---

[9] Timothy Keller, *The Grand Demythologizer: The Gospel and Idolatry*, The Gospel Coalition 2009 National Conference, https://vimeo.com/5834236

discuss the discerning, exposing, and challenging the idols of our surrounding culture through gospel ministry. Idolatry surprises me, time and time again startling me with its craftiness. When I walked away from feminism to a patriarchal model of gender roles, I assumed that I was walking away from the obsession with "I am an intelligent and undeniably independent woman, hear me roar!" Devouring one book after another on biblical womanhood, how to be an excellent wife, how to dress demurely, how to be quiet (I had a hard time with that one), how to be meek, how to have a traditional family, how to apply myself to domesticity with excellence, and on and on, I thought that I was correcting my previous faulty notions of womanhood. When God in his grace lifted the blindness of gospel amnesia and in his mercy drove me to open my ears to someone like Tim Keller who has a gift for discerning, exposing and challenging people's idols, I saw that I may have moved philosophical positions, but my idol had stayed the same, it just took on a different form: I was still obsessed with being a woman. Now it was "I am a biblical and unquestioningly submissive woman, hear me roar!" It's hard to relate in words the spiritual experience of having such an idol revealed to oneself.

Womanhood can be, and often is, an idol for many. Whether framed in the image of feminist activists, authors, or media personalities on one side, *or* the Proverbs 31 woman as she is or as we imagine her, whether an admired friend, neighbor, or pastor's wife, or whatever form it takes on in our peculiar subculture, ultimately we are susceptible to glorying in womanhood more than in Christ. It is the same for men, I might add. Men can also come to idolize manhood. Frankly, it doesn't matter if it's "biblical" or otherwise, no created thing is to be idolized and the creature may never be worshiped.

Another devastating idol discerned and exposed was spiritual maturity. What I called "godliness" had become an idol for me at this time because I saw it as a way of being "better" than other people, very much like the Pharisee in Luke 18:9–12:

> He also told this parable to some who trusted in themselves that they were righteous and treated others with contempt. Two men went up into the temple to pray, one a Pharisee and the other a tax collector. The Pharisee standing by himself, prayed thus: God, I thank you that I am not like other men, extortioners, unjust, adulterers, or even like this tax collector. I fast twice a week; I give tithes of all that I get.

Setting my personal preferences and convictions as sanctification markers by which to judge other people, caused me to look with contempt at those "tax collectors" around me. I also believed that God would love me more if I were more spiritually mature. These two idols in particular are very painful for me to remember.

The gospel, on the other hand, tells me that my primary identity is in Christ. The love that I long for is mine supremely in the cross work of Jesus. The cross admits no idols, but our Lord has grace and patience with us as we figure this out.

When "[we] look to a created thing to give [us] something that only God can give [us], that's idolatry.[10]" In the case of those of us who had or have gospel amnesia we can look to many "good" things to give us what only God can give us. In my life all those years, I looked to many things, even to social standing in my church culture, the sacraments, church traditions, particular orders of liturgy in the church worship service, religious activity, and the nitty-gritty of doctrinal views. (Your list may be different than mine.) I didn't treat these things just as good things (which they can be if they are a genuine outworking of the gospel), I acted as if they were *ultimate things*. They were markers to gauge my spiritual growth and the sanctification level of others in the church, near and far.

It's too easy for us Christians to think of idolatry as a sin exclusive to the unbeliever. Idolatry is a foundational sin for all humans. Therefore, Christian and non-Christian alike need the gospel preached in such a way that hearts will be exposed and challenged and idols confronted and destroyed. This was one of Keller's points in *The Grand Demythologizer*: every religion has its idols, every culture has its idols, every gender has its idols, ever race has its idols. The job of gospel ministry is to discern, expose and destroy these idols. Only then will we see heart transformation rather than behavior

---

[10] Ibid

modification. It is this kind of transformation which will make us a gracious and sober minded people, offering ourselves through spiritual worship as living sacrifices, holy and acceptable to God (Rom.12:1–3)

Something very subtle happens when we have gospel amnesia: we may become convinced that we are free from heart-idolatry. The reason we believe this is not so much that we think we are sinless, but because we are not gospel-conscious. Discerning, exposing, and destroying idols is an *intrinsic function* of the gospel as applied by the Holy Spirit. We wrongly conclude that since we may not be captivated by beauty, sophistry, power, celebrity or money—the idols we claim are worshiped by our culture—than we must be idolatry-free. We dismiss or diminish our "clean" idols—all those good things we trust in to save us and our children to make us "clean." Christians can have many idols: Doctrinal pharisaism can be an idol, morality can be an idol, penning harsh and mocking words towards others in defense of the faith can be an idol, apologetics can be an idol, ministry in the church can be an idol, hospitality can be an idol, a charismatic or celebrity pastor can be an idol, really just about anything can be an idol. Our hearts are deceptive, and unless we are overpowered by the grace and the glory of God through self-conscious gospel immersion, we can become ensnared to almost anything.

Lastly, we have a temptation to quickly see the idolatry of others around us while turning a blind eye to our own. This is dangerous to the soul and is another symptom of a heart that isn't being washed and sharpened by the gospel. It is easier for those of us with gospel amnesia to spot someone obsessed with their physical health and beauty than it is to notice that we have elevated the long denim skirt as the *sine qua non* of biblical womanhood. My hypocrisy in this area still grieves me. I grieve for people I scoffed at and judged instead of reaching out to; I grieve for modeling such a repugnant Christianity to my children, for time wasted on pettiness and trivialities, and I grieve for the sins I laid up in my heart. I had cast aside the precious cross, the gospel—the good news that I thought I was too mature to preach to myself daily. The triad of distraction, progression, and presumption kept me in bondage. May the Lord Jesus forgive me and may these simple entreaties I write be used by the Holy Spirit to remove blindness and pierce hearts.

It is certainly right to classify idolatry as a Distraction Mode of gospel amnesia, but we should recognize that our idols can just as easily be idols of Progression or Presumption. Our idols forge their way to the center of the life of our soul requiring total homage and worship; distracting us from who *He* is and what *He* has done and who we are in relation to *Him*. Their distraction need not be total for them to be effective; Screwtape considers any diminution of Christ in our minds to be gain, and when all these little idols together ever so slightly edge out Christ, the deceiver claims a victory.

LOSING THE TENSION BETWEEN TRANSCENDENCE AND IMMANENCE: A SYMPTOM OF GOSPEL AMNESIA

I remember during the years when I had forgotten the gospel, I talked a lot about God, his laws, and striving to obey him and working out our salvation with fear and trembling. I would use the word "Lord" a lot. I rarely, if ever, spoke or thought about Jesus, God the Son. With my theologically truncated and flattened view of the gospel, Christ took on an auxiliary role. Life was about living faithfully to biblical principles, even daily Bible reading was about being "obedient" and "godly." I didn't see that the center of Scripture was Christ. Christ had a key role, to be sure, but that was all, he was only one part, albeit a crucial part of God's plan and kingdom. I flattened the newness and goodness of the new covenant.

God is majestic, high and lifted up, *and* he is near and present on earth and with his people. He is both of these things *at all times*. In theological terms we use words like transcendence and immanence to describe these two aspects of God. In a way, we see the entirety of the Bible speaking of God's immanence (his presence) within his creation, even though he is distinct from it. If, like I did, we start weighing one part of his attributes more than another, we can start unhinging the different parts of God, even while earnestly trying to understand him.

Partly (although not completely) because of the disrespectful way I would hear Christians speak about

God, like he is their boyfriend, I fell into an overcorrection in this area. Because I had let the gospel grow dim and was not in the least dwelling on it or filtering things through it, I fell into weighing heavily the transcendence of God and diminished to almost nothing God's immanence. I was very much into speaking highly of God and thinking of him as King and Lord. In my mind he was always on his throne, high and lifted up, majestic, worthy of all reverence and respect. The thought of a "personal relationship with Jesus" repelled me. I saw it as a degradation of his Lordship. I tended to neglect the times that I yearned for his nearness as a throw-back to an immature emotion—thereby robbing myself of intimacy with the Spirit.

Because we are made in the *image* of God to be *worshipers* of God, we are made with a desire for both his closeness *and* majesty—his immanence *and* transcendence. What we see in Jesus is the Incarnation of *both* of these qualities. He is both Immanuel (God with us) and Kurios (absolute sovereign Lord). In Jesus, transcendence and immanence kiss.

When the gospel slips from our horizon, who Jesus is and what he did becomes distant—acknowledged but not spiritually sensed. When we develop gospel amnesia, no matter how much we think we are attending to God's transcendence, we lose sight and awareness of his nearness—his presence.

BOREDOM WITH THE GOSPEL: A SYMPTOM OF GOSPEL AMNESIA

I remember many times over the years, but especially right before our move to Arizona, telling my husband that I did *not* want a church that was all about Jesus. I told him that I didn't want to hear every Sunday about how Jesus died for our sins. I said that that was too evangelistic, and besides, I was already a Christian. I saw churches and church cultures that spoke that way as participating in an immature and superficial Christianity. I remember thinking that as a mature Christian I should not be spending my time on Jesus. After all, he is the foundation; he is the basics. We learn about Jesus in Sunday School; we learn him and then move on. This type of boredom falls squarely under the Progression Mode of gospel amnesia—we've moved on, progressed from the message of the gospel.

Are you tired of hearing about Jesus? Do you ever secretly say to yourself deep in your heart: "Okay, I got it already, I'm sick of it, I'm bored with it, can we move on, please?" Are you at a point in your life where you are rarely moved in the soul? Is it possible that you are the lukewarm drink mentioned in Rev. 3:15–17? If you have thought or are thinking along these lines then maybe a reflection on gospel amnesia can be a turning point for you. If you are not careful, the tendency will be to finish this book and think, "Okay, got it, now I also know what gospel amnesia is about," filing it away in your spiritual categories and moving on.

Boredom with the gospel is one ramification of gospel

amnesia. I have heard it said that if *you* are bored with the gospel, the problem is *not* with the gospel. This is true, but it does not go far enough in helping those who do find themselves in this situation for one reason or another. Why does this happen to Christians? The simple answer to this is sin, of course. But what is beneath this particular manifestation of sin? In this section I want to tackle three underlying reasons: Neglecting the infinitude of God, the perception of repetition, and a hazy or weak understanding of the atonement.

NEGLECTING THE INFINITUDE OF GOD

The triune God—Father, Son, and Holy Spirit—is infinite. Anyone who has learned mathematics beyond basic arithmetic can tell you that the concept of infinity is hard for the human mind to grapple with. We tend to either ignore its hugeness, or think that we have mastered it simply by defining it. When we think of infinitude, it may help to meditate on other words such as: boundless, without limit, without restriction, beyond measurement, bottomless, and so on. However, *if we deemphasize God's infinitude, then the gospel shrinks in our minds*. The gospel is inextricably tied to God's infinitude *because the grace shown in the gospel is infinite*. The chasm God breached in calling us to him from our state of sin is infinite. The capacity of Christ to reverse sin, disease, decay, entropy itself—is infinite.

Once the gospel shrinks in our minds, it doesn't take much to imagine bounds on it and make it finite. Once it is finite it is easy to recreate it in our image and make it man-sized. Once it becomes man-sized, we think we have understood all there is to understand of it. The end result: Boredom with a tamed, domesticated, one-dimensional flattened gospel.

It is amazing to me that God allows us to know him. Special revelation (God's speaking to us through his prophets and apostles in Scripture) is a beautiful condescension on his part. Unfortunately, this is another area in which I slipped. There is something deceiving (at least it was for me anyway) about having the ability to read and gain knowledge about God. Whether it is Scripture reading or theological reading, this God-given invitation to learn about God can fool us into thinking we *can* know *everything* about him. When we are not daily washing our minds with the gospel, we forget how infinite he is, and we forget how finite we actually are. That old pride from the garden that thinks we can know as he knows is always with us, tempting us to have a high view of our own understanding while reducing God to *our man-sized knowability*.

THE PERCEPTION OF REPETITION

If the *presentation* one receives of the gospel is repetitive in its form, then it can give a person the illusion that the topic itself is repetitive. To paraphrase one of Tim Keller's observations:[11] If a teacher understands the gospel to be "the basics," and

---

[11] Timothy Keller, *Pragmatism, Progressivism, & Moralism,* The Gospel Coalition http://thegospelcoalition.org/resources/entry/pragmatism_progressivism_moralism

preaching is understood chiefly as a way to tell people how to live (expounding biblical principles), then the unsaved are bored and confused because they have no reason to pay attention to a God who is merely the author of biblical principles. However, if the gospel is preached as if it is primarily about the basic elementary doctrines people need to know to become a Christian, then the saved are bored because when they hear it, they sit in the pews thinking: "My soul is already saved, okay already!"

If we understand that all human problems at a heart level are a lack of resting in and believing the gospel for Christians and non-Christians alike,[12] then the gospel will be preached every week no matter where in Scripture the pastor is preaching from. Properly spoken, the gospel is both saving and preserving, both calling and instructing. No one will be bored, the unbelievers will get evangelized and the believers will get edified. The gospel is not a set of elementary doctrines just to get people to become Christians, nor is it the expounding of principles telling people how to live.[13] The real gospel has power: real, supernatural, transformative power. The real gospel is the kingdom of God being kneaded in, and throughout, the world.

A WEAK ATONEMENT

Letting the Savior be the Savior was a constant struggle for me. I put too much faith in what I was bringing with

---

[12] Ibid

[13] Ibid

my striving for obedience. Unfortunately, neither my works nor my sacrifices could atone for my sins. "But God, being rich in mercy, because of the great love with which he loved [me], even when [I] [was] dead in [my] trespasses, made [me] alive together with Christ... For by grace [I] have been saved through faith. And this is not [my] own doing; it is the gift of God, not a result of works, so that [I do not] boast" (Eph. 2:4, 8–9). And now he equips me for this work (Eph. 4:12).

Because of God's *justice*, Jesus had to come, live, and die. Because of God's *love*, Jesus had to come, live, die, and live again. (Rom. 3:25–26, John 3:16) The punishment deserved by me, Jesus Christ bore in *full measure*—to the last dregs—in his body on the tree. (1 Peter 2:24) He was made to be like me (his brethren) in every respect so that he might become a merciful and faithful high priest. (Heb. 2:17) This willingness of Christ scares me. If God the Son was willing "for the joy that was set before him" to do what he did, then what ramifications should this have in my heart? If no penance, works, or sacrifice on my part can take away my sins and help Jesus out even a tiny bit, where does that leave me?

Distracted by the sacrifices and the works I had to perform for my idols, and looking for a holiness that was more holy than Christ, nothing could wean me from self-sufficiency other than the loving chastening of a holy, good and righteous heavenly Father. (Soul perseverance is entirely a work of God.) No more could I look at my deeds. I needed the deeds of another—a better sacrifice was required (Heb. 9:23). Only the blood of Jesus, a "sacrifice of infinite worth and value, abundantly sufficient to expiate [my sins]",[14] could atone for me. Even now in my ever restless desire to please God, to earn *something* so that he would love and delight in me, I must constantly remind myself that my heavenly Father already loves and delights in me. This, because of the life and death of Jesus. Jesus is infinitely worthy, infinitely beautiful, infinitely pleasing to the Father. But what about my obedience? Well, my obedience used to be backwards. I would trumpet John 14:15 talking about how people who really loved God obeyed his commandments. For me, *obeying meant loving.* In his sermon, *If Anyone Loves Me He Will Keep My Word*, John Piper says something very profound. It is something many who struggle with the love of God and the atoning work of Christ need to internalize: "loving Jesus is not the same as keeping his commandments. It precedes and gives rise to keeping the commandments. Keeping his word is the *result* of loving him, not the *same* as loving him."[15] (Emphases in the original) This piece of wisdom completely revolutionizes the way someone with gospel amnesia thinks about obedience to God. Something very subtle happens in our hearts when we think that obedience *means* love: we obey to get God to respond to us, to love us back and to bless us. So how should we think about

---

[14] Herman Bavinck, *Reformed Dogmatics: Abridged In One Volume* (Michigan: Baker Academic, 2011) 462

[15] John Piper, *If Anyone Loves Me He Will Keep My Word*, Desiring God http://www.desiringgod.org/resource-library/sermons/if-anyone-loves-me-he-will-keep-my-word

obedience in light of this? Obey out of love *for* him—
yes! Obey to get love *from* him—no!

Our puny reductionistic understanding may think of Jesus' suffering as only his time on the cross, or perhaps starting with his trial, or if we're feeling particularly expansive, the whole window of time between his arrest and when he sat up before walking out of the tomb. However, the profundity and complexity of the gospel shows us (if we have eyes to see) that Christ suffered throughout his life. Every time he was spoken ill of, every time his motives were questioned, every lie and misjudgment of his character was an infinite breach of cosmic justice, going beyond any slights we incur upon our own egos. He took on the fullness of human suffering. He was "a man of sorrows, and acquainted with grief" (Isa. 53:3).

The gospel of Jesus Christ—which includes scourging, flogging, torn open flesh rubbing against wood, nails in the wrists, nails in the feet, suffocation and a crown of thorns—is no light and fluffy gospel cushioning us from hardship and giving us a safe and ordered life. Ours is a bloody gospel, good news that plucks our souls out of everlasting darkness into everlasting light in the presence of God. That is what the gospel does—brings us into the presence of God where we shout with angels and the elders around the throne:

> Worthy is the lamb who was slain, to receive power and wealth, and wisdom and might and honor and glory and blessing! — Rev. 5:12

What about you, are you gripped by the cross? John Piper has said, "Nothing is more foundational for the joy of undeserving people than then the cross of Jesus Christ."[16] Since it was rare for me to *feel* undeserving (because of my performance), I had a real problem when it came to the cross. But if it were not for the cross, we would all certainly perish. We plead his propitiation. This means that as Christians we should be exulting in the atonement—the work Christ did in his life and death to earn our salvation.[17]

Why are the reasons for boredom with the gospel important? As I mentioned in chapter one, Progression Mode is a form of gospel amnesia. *It is this mode in particular that promotes boredom with the gospel and lukewarmness.* Progression Mode does *not* equal intellectual conceit. Gospel amnesia is no respecter of intelligence, it doesn't matter how "smart" you are; we can all get gospel amnesia. This manifestation is very old; it goes all the way back to the Garden—its root is pride. From the beginning we have wanted to be like God and desired to progress from our need of God. The gospel shows us how small and needy we are. The gospel is all about what God has done in the life and death of Jesus Christ. We don't like that. We don't want to dwell on *that*. "That's nice," we say, "meh." Like our first parents back in the Garden, we want to gain the knowledge and move on.

---

[16] Thanks to Tony Reinke for pointing me to this statement and to the John Piper sermon *Boasting Only In The Cross*

[17] Wayne Grudem, *Systematic Theology: An Introduction To Biblical Doctrine* (Michigan: Zondervan, 1994) 568

A TRUNCATED VIEW OF THE GOSPEL: A ROOT OF GOSPEL AMNESIA

A truncated or reductionistic view of the gospel can and does lead to gospel amnesia. D.A. Carson has said many times that one of our problems is that we think the gospel is only for tipping us into the kingdom and after that we think we need to move on to how to parent and how to disciple and how to go about doing a lot of Christianly things. I am calling this a one-dimensional, or flattened gospel. These reductionistic thoughts of what God has done in Christ Jesus lead straight to gospel amnesia.

In this view, the gospel is distilled down to a handful of propositional truths. We take these truths and intellectually assent to them—calling them the "milk" of the faith—and then boastfully say we are moving on (in Progression) to the "meat." However, when we assume that only the milk is "Jesus" and that the meat/solid food is supposed to be something *more* than that, we have subverted the person and work of God the Son, and superimposed our human wisdom onto biblical wisdom. Yet, like so many errors, it is formed around a kernel of truth. Intellectual assent isn't enough; Intellectual assent doesn't have transformative power. If the gospel truly was a mere proposition, it *would* leave us wanting and seeking more.

The meat of Scripture is maturation, further up and into, the theology and practice of the love of Jesus Christ; growing up into the fullness of Christ. (1 Peter 2:1–2) Jesus Christ only is to be worshiped and glorified. But our hearts can subtly dethrone Jesus for something *we consider* to be more substantial—"meatier." In our quest for Christian maturity we come to think Jesus is not enough for us. We are stumbled by the simplicity of the gospel. Soon, in our desire for more, we look to other things to make us *feel like* we are growing or maturing. As we scan the Evangelical landscape we see a variety of manifestations: For some it is reading heavy theological tomes and sitting around smoking cigars discussing fine categorical distinctions. For others it is natural and "biblical" nutrition, the ministry of missions, the ministry to the poor, neo-agrarianism and so on. (For the sake of clarity, let me point out that gospel amnesia is not an affliction of the doctrinally conservative only. Everything I have said and will say can be applied to those in doctrinally liberal circles, it just takes on a different form.) There is a tendency for us to be deceived into thinking that these things in themselves are the "meat" of the Christian life and that Jesus is merely the "milk." This is what it looks like to have a truncated one-dimensional flattened gospel: Jesus is reduced to being the door, or the foundation, or the "milk," or the "basics," and then… we move on.

In reference to Hebrews 5:11–14, concerning the milk and solid food, Matthew Henry says this:

> The apostle shows how the various doctrines of the gospel must be dispensed to different persons. There are in the church babes and persons of full age (v. 12–14), and *there are in the gospel milk and*

strong meat.[18] (Emphasis mine)

The point here is that the gospel is *everything,* dispensed to each listener according to where they are spiritually, when it is preached faithfully by pastors through the work and the ministry of the Holy Spirit. It is *not* that Jesus is the milk and then we move on to biblical principles as if they are the solid food, as I used to hold.

In the end, anything that usurps Jesus in our minds and deceives us into thinking that we are becoming more sanctified, even *if* those things are good biblical principles, is in actuality making us *forget* the gospel. It is good to want spiritual meat; it is good to want to grow in our faith, but that happens when we constantly keep the gospel before our eyes. The gospel is a balanced meal... It is both the milk and the meat! The gospel manifests itself as milk for the new believer, and that same gospel manifests itself as meat for the spiritually mature. But it is the Holy Spirit Himself which takes the gospel of Christ and uses it to comfort, sharpen, prune, convict, and adorn the believer.

The Apostle Peter puts it this way:

> So put away all malice and all deceit and hypocrisy and envy and all slander (evil speaking). Like newborn infants, *long for the pure spiritual milk, that by it you may grow up into salvation.* 1 Peter

---

[18] Matthew Henry, *Matthew Henry's Commentary on the Whole Bible Complete and Unabridged* (Hendrickson Publishers, LLC, 1991), 2388

2:1–2 (Emphasis mine)

I am not calling for an immaturity here, any more than Peter was. To the contrary, I am trying to expose our faulty thinking behind what we call growth. True spiritual growth does not happen outside the horizon of the gospel. It is the gospel that *sanctifies* as well as *justifies*. All those years when I had gospel amnesia I fooled myself into thinking I was becoming more mature as a Christian because I had a certain outward adherence but I was what Jesus calls a "whitewashed tomb." I was busy cleaning the "outside of the cup and plate" indulging petty righteousness; While I neglected the weightier matters of the law: justice, mercy, and faithfulness (Matthew 23:23).

This and so much more, used to be my life, but God had other plans for me, and as Jerry Bridges put it, "gradually over time, and from a deep sense of need, I came to realize that the gospel is for believers too." The Holy Spirit has been a palpable presence in my life since that day of spiritual renaissance. His work has come in waves. This was the extraordinary work of God in the heart and spirit of an ordinary sinner. I merited none of it. This spiritual renewal did not come to me because I was more pious than others, or because I was somehow more worthy in God's economy. There is no me in this! It was completely and purely the supernatural work of God based solely on his immeasurable grace.

What has become the center of your individual life?

QUESTIONS

Spend time meditating on your idols. We all have them. Ask the Holy Spirit to lift the veil of your heart and expose your idols to you. Then pray for the Lord to destroy your idols.

How do you think about God? Spend some time dwelling on the trinitarian nature of God. Consider reading a book on the Trinity. Ask the Holy Spirit to give you a desire for the presence of Christ. Practice his presence. Ask the Holy Spirit to exercise your spiritual senses.

When do you get tired of hearing about the gospel? Do you get tired of hearing the gospel?

Consider studying the doctrine of atonement. Dwell on the fullness of the cross work of Christ.

When someone says the word "gospel" or when you hear the word "gospel" what do you feel? What are the first thoughts that come to your mind?

PRAYER

Most merciful Father, I come poor, tattered, and sick. I confess my lack of desire for you. I confess that there are times when I don't care about what you have done and what you are doing. Your Word does not move my soul. I confess that I have a long list of desires, all of which excite me so much more than spending time with you in prayer and reading your Word. Yet, I know that

Jesus paid for my cold heart along with my blasphemous thoughts, on that cross. Jesus died for my lack of desire. Jesus died for my selfishness. Jesus died so that the Holy Spirit can indwell me and give me a fervent desire for you. I believe, Lord, help my unbelief. Fill me with your Holy Spirit and quicken my heart so that my desire for you is insatiable. Amen.

CHAPTER THREE:

Gospel Amnesia & the Local Church

What has become the center for you in your local church?

I am sure there are many ways gospel amnesia manifests itself in the local church. I will touch on a few areas, which in my experience I see as the most damaging to ourselves, our brothers and sisters, and the overall unity of a local body of believers.

SPIRITUAL COVETEOUSNESS AND SPIRITUAL PRIDE: A SYMPTOM OF GOSPEL AMNESIA

A few years ago I watched one of my dear friends start maturing and growing spiritually. There seemed to be a tangible difference in the way she served her family and in the way she related to her husband. This was not an act; the Lord was working in my friend's life. Instead of rejoicing with her and seeking to learn from her, I became envious. I told myself that it was okay, that we are allowed as Christians to "covet" someone else's sanctification because it would drive us to try hard and do better and become more spiritually mature ourselves. This was at the height of my gospel amnesia years and I was in my Progression Mode, I had "moved on" from the gospel and was busy growing and becoming "more sanctified" with all those "right things" I was doing. Except that I wasn't growing, my heart was becoming darkened with envy. I actually envied my friend's spiritual growth; I wanted it for myself, and not in addition to her, but *instead* of her! Is that not sick with sin? How very Cain-like of me. If that's not gospel amnesia, I'm not sure what is. It grieves me deeply when I think about how sick my heart was that I would resent the work of the Holy Spirit in my friend's life.

This went on for almost an entire year until one day I couldn't take the conviction from the Sprit any longer. This sin was crushing me. I called my friend and admitted everything. Of course she forgave me. It's not like my poor friend hadn't noticed that I had been irritable with her for almost a year, but she waited patiently for me to come talk to her. She was very longsuffering, way more than I had ever been with her, to my shame.

This type of sin is real in the local church and it needs to be brought into the light. As long as we keep our "little" sins hidden in the dark we have no hope of overcoming and standing victorious over them. The entire time I was being eaten by envy over my friend's spiritual growth, my longsuffering friend had been praying for me. She saw that I was in bondage. I will dare to say that gospel amnesia is that—bondage.

Have you ever felt ashamed or guilty because you can't seem to keep up with someone else's sanctification? On the other side: have you ever let words slip from your lips (e.g. how many times a week you do family worship, what books you are reading, which parenting and education method you are using, etc.) to show how far along your family is on the sanctification spectrum? In other words, have you ever "preached Christ" out of envy, rivalry, or selfish ambition (Philippians 1:15–17)? I certainly have.

Spiritual covetousness and spiritual pride are real, and can do damage to relationships and to a church body. These are subtle sins. Nourished by the fertile soil of a gospel amnesic church culture, they creep into hearts under the guise of the call to "let us consider how to stir up one another to love and good works" (Hebrews 10:24). They manifest themselves in a myriad of ways across countless personalities. How does this type of thing happen? How do we get to a point in the local body where we resent the work of the Holy Spirit in someone else's life, or sling around our spiritual pride provoking our brethren? How do we forget that it was he who said, "I will have mercy on whom I will have mercy, and I will have compassion on whom I will have compassion?"[19] The answer is: Gospel amnesia. We forget the gospel and the cross at the heart of the gospel. We forget the work of Christ.

The local church is a messy place; a place full of sinners in need of their savior every day. You and I are part of this organism. Hence, if we personally have gospel amnesia, we can imagine how that could exponentiate

---

[19] See discussion of the use of Exodus 33:19 in Romans 9:15 in *Commentary on the New Testament Use of the Old Testament*, G.K. Beale and D.A. Carson (Michigan: Baker Academic, 2007), 641–643

within the local body. Here too we have to ask ourselves: What has become the center of our local church? What excites those in the pews around us?

LACK OF CHARITY TOWARD FELLOW CHRISTIANS: A SYMPTOM OF GOSPEL AMNESIA

One of the ways gospel amnesia manifests itself is in charity toward Christian liberty. Charity, toward other (different) Christians, was rarely a fruit of my heart during the gospel amnesia years. Whether it was despising my brethren, or judging their entertainment choices, parenting methods, educational methods, or even their view of the Lord's Day—Sunday (I used to be a strict Sabbatarian). No matter the category, I had all the "biblical" answers. Charity toward the brethren has fallen on hard times in the lives of many believers, one can see this by perusing the internet or counting the number of Christian micro-denominations. Scripture makes clear that charity is a principal thing; it is not a secondary issue. We don't get to say, "I think I'll skip charity, it's not for me." This would be laughable if it wasn't sadly true. Jesus spoke his harshest words against people like me, pharisees "opting out" of charity.

We might read through the 14th chapter of Romans and nod, thinking: "yes, yes, those poor foolish Gentiles getting worked up over meat and vegetables and feast days." This scoffing attitude reveals our blindness. We glibly scan over the chapter and move on thinking we've got this down (Progression Mode). Today's believers may not be quarreling over meat and vegetables but we are just as disposed to bite and devour one another over other secondary matters. This is exactly what gospel amnesia does—marginalizes the gospel and sets up a secondary issue as center. And then we start warring.

Some years back, in studying Romans 14, I noticed that there is a way to test oneself to see whether on any particular issue we are like a weaker brother or a stronger brother. The reason this is important is not just because we are to grow out of our weaknesses under the tutelage of the Holy Spirit through gospel-centered, Christ-exalting teaching, but because each of these has a particular temptation or sin they fall into. When we identify our temptation and/or sin the gospel calls us to address the heart problem: repenting and seeking the Holy Spirit's help to obey this portion of Scripture:

> As for the one who is weak in faith, welcome him, but not to quarrel over opinions. One person believes he may eat anything, while the weak person eats only vegetables. Let not the one who eats *despise* the one who abstains, and let not the one who abstains *pass judgment* on the one who eats, for God has welcomed him. Who are you to pass judgment on the servant of another? It is before his own master that he stand or falls. And he will be upheld, for the Lord is able to make him stand. Romans 14:1–4 (Emphases mine)

A prima facie reading of the text tells us there are

strong faith Christians and weak faith Christians and that the stronger brother should welcome the weaker one without quarreling over matters of opinion. Paul assumes here that *there are indeed things in the Christian life that are a matter of opinion.* For those of us overcoming gospel amnesia, we may remember with sorrow how we had raised all kinds of issues to primary, nearly salvific, importance. We see by implication of the text that the weaker brother is not to snub and/or refuse and/or run away from table fellowship with the stronger brother. The two are not to quarrel over opinions. As a caveat: When we attach ourselves to certain distinctives, and if they become our identity, our gospel amnesic hearts can very quickly set these secondary issues as sanctification markers for other people's spiritual growth. This is sin. Once we start thinking that a brother or sister, after believing in Jesus, must also adhere to our hobby horse issues, not for maturation, but for genuineness, then we are telling them that Jesus is not sufficient. However, as Don Carson warns, "The Word of God will not allow anyone or anything to jeopardize the exclusive sufficiency of Jesus."[20]

Verse two says that the *stronger* brother "believes he may eat anything, while the *weak* person eats only vegetables." The weak Christian, as Don Carson puts it, is "someone who has sensitivities to right and wrong *even though* in the issue itself it's not a matter of right

---

[20] D.A. Carson, *That By All Means I Might Win Some: Faithfulness and Flexibility in Gospel Proclamation (1Cor. 9:19–23)*, The Gospel Coalition 2009 National Conference http://thegospelcoalition.org/resources/entry/That-By-All-Means-I-Might-Win-Some

and wrong."[21] If we apply the principle here to any type of secondary subject (e.g. drinking wine & spirits, forms of church liturgy, instruments in the worship service, education methods for children, etc.) we see that the stronger Christian has a *broader acceptable spectrum*, whereas the weaker brother has a *narrow understanding of what is acceptable or right*. This is key here, because these perspectives (broad or narrow) on the different issues in life, are critical to grace-based relationships within the local church. We must remember from other sections of Scripture that Paul is very concerned with preserving the integrity of the individual conscience,[22] so by no means is he suggesting for the stronger brother to get pushy and pressure the weaker brother into a position which makes him harden his conscience. We see this as we read on in Romans 14. "Paul doesn't want you to harm your conscience even if your conscience is so weak it is ill-informed about what is right or wrong."[23]

To be clear, Paul is not talking about sin issues in this passage. It does not imply that someone with ultimately strong faith would tolerate *all* things, but we can assume that the grace with which they would handle confrontations with true sin would be in the mold of Christ, who lived with and confronted sinners every day

---

[21] D.A. Carson, *That By All Means I Might Win Some: Faithfulness and Flexibility in Gospel Proclamation (1Cor. 9:19–23)*, The Gospel Coalition 2009 National Conference http://thegospelcoalition.org/resources/entry/That-By-All-Means-I-Might-Win-Some

[22] Ibid

[23] Ibid

of his time on Earth. It also bears repeating that the logical implication in Romans 14 is that those with strong faith will have broader acceptance, *not* that those with broad acceptance of things have stronger faith. We can easily find examples of people with broad acceptance of things who have little or no faith. That isn't the point. The broader tolerance of a strong Christian (proper biblical tolerance) is actually an overflowing of grace, and its source is God himself.

Verse three mentions two specific sins we can fall into: despising and passing judgment. Notice that the stronger brother's sin or temptation is to *despise* his weaker brother and the weaker brother's sin and/or temptation is to *pass judgment* on his stronger brother. You don't need to have full blown gospel amnesia like I did to be a critical person, despising those on the one side and passing judgement on the choices of those on the other side. Any setting up of our personal convictions and standards as the watermark of sanctification for our fellow brethren is forbidden by Scripture. Any forgetting of the gospel will do it, any turning away from the charity we are called to have for one another—any lack of grace in the heart will turn us into people who look sideways at each other. Jesus said that the litmus test for being his disciples before the world was this:

> By this all people will know that you are my disciples, if you have love for one another. John 13:35

Looking at a few more verses in Romans 14:

> Each one should be fully convinced *in his own mind*. Romans 14:5 (Emphasis mine)

> Why do you *pass judgment* on your brother? Or you, why do you *despise* your brother? *For we will all stand before the judgment seat of God*; for it is written, 'As I live, says the Lord, every knee shall bow to me, and every tongue shall confess to God.' So then each of us will give an account of himself to God. Romans 14:10–12 (Emphases mine)

> I know and am persuaded in the Lord Jesus that *nothing is unclean in itself,* but it is unclean for anyone who thinks it unclean. Romans 14:14 (Emphases mine)

> So then let us pursue what makes for peace and for mutual upbuilding. Romans 14:19

> ... For whatever does not proceed from faith is sin. Romans 14:23

Taking in the above verses, let me throw out a hypothetical: When we stand before the judgment seat of Almighty God (who is a consuming fire), are we going to talk to him about the way Suzy–Q dressed and how she only had one kid and she sent him to public school and went off to work, or how Bobby–Joe had three piercings and five tattoos, or how Joe–Shmoe "polluted" Sunday morning worship by playing the electric guitar and drums? Of course not! We will be trembling in fear and adoration before our Holy God, and so will Suzy-Q, Bobby-Joe and Joe-Shmoe. So why then do we continue to strain gnats and swallow camels? Jesus said, "Go and learn what this means, 'I desire mercy, and not sacrifice'" Matthew 9:13. "And if you had known what this means, 'I desire mercy, and not sacrifice,' you would not have condemned the guiltless" Matthew 12:7. I grieve in my spirit when I remember how I have condemned the guiltless.

Jerry Bridges in *Transforming Grace* says:

> As Christians we can't seem to accept the clear biblical teaching in Romans 14 that God allows equally godly people to have differing opinions on certain matters. We universalize what we think is God's particular leading in our lives and apply it to everyone else... Even if you believe God has led you in developing those convictions, you still must not elevate them to the level of spiritual principles for everyone else to follow. The respected Puritan theologian John Owen taught that 'only what God has commanded in his word should be regarded as binding: in all else there may be liberty of actions.' If we are going to enjoy the freedom we have in Christ, we must be alert to convictions that fall into the category of differing opinions. We must not seek to bind the consciences of others or allow them to bind ours. We must stand firm in the freedom we have in Christ.

If there is an injunction by which we find ourselves conscience-bound, but that we can only find in scripture by making lots of definitions or tracing back through long chains of implications, let us admit that we *might* be the weaker brother on that issue. In any case, we do not need to necessarily give up our convictions so much as hold them with humility. Let us allow that true Christian brethren can in good faith and conscience differ, and do not pass judgment on them. Brethren, let us strive for the things that make for peace. As one who has been blind and is seeking the grace to practice all these things, I recommend meditating on Romans 15:5–7

> May the God of endurance and encouragement grant you to live in such harmony with one another, in accord with Christ Jesus, that together you may with one voice glorify the God and Father of our Lord Jesus Christ. Therefore welcome one another as Christ has welcomed you, for the glory of God. Romans 15:5–7

SINS IN THE LOCAL CHURCH

There is sin in every church, because every church, no matter how small or how selective, is made up of fallen humans.

Gospel amnesia flourishes in a local church where there is a disconnect between doctrine and culture. An obvious case would be a church where there is no gospel preaching. Another would be a church that is obligation-heavy and gospel-light. Yet another is where there is a fair amount of gospel doctrine with little or no gospel action.

Ray Ortlund Jr. asks in *Justification versus Self-Justification,* "what kind of dark church culture can a mentality of self-justification (*gospel amnesia*)[24] create?" Here are some of his answers: Selfish ambition, manipulative power of exclusion, a sense of grievance toward some, a redefining of what it takes to be an acceptable Christian (a "Jesus + Something" mentality), biting, devouring, insecurity, anxiety, fear and anger. I would add suspicion, warring over secondary matters, verbal or non-verbal pressure to adhere to unstated rules, a culture of affectation, preoccupation with outward behavior, and a lack of humility and transparency. A church rife with gospel amnesia can trumpet all day long that they hold to the gospel, but if the fruit of church culture shows otherwise, they have effectively de-gospeled the gospel.[25]

When members of a church are blinded by gospel amnesia, dealing with sin in the congregation is hampered by a lack of grace and a gospel-centered rebuke and restoration process. How can a people tackle difficulties in their relationships and in their

---

[24] Ray Ortlund Jr., "Justification versus Self-Justification," (Paper presented at The Gospel Coalition National Conference, April 13, 2011)

[25] My deep gratitude to Pastor Ray Ortlund Jr. whose talk, *Justification versus Self-Justification* helped me to crystalize some of these thoughts. His phrase "de-gospel the gospel" had me taking notes feverishly while driving and listening.

body life when they have forgotten the gospel, Jesus has been marginalized, and the center has become many things, none of which is the gospel and cross work of Christ!?

The friend I mentioned in the beginning of the chapter has long since forgiven me. Although we went through more hard times, the Lord has always brought us back together. I will say this: The only reason our relationship survived such heavy sinning was due purely to the cross of Jesus. When the two of us grabbed hold of the gospel again, when we started understanding the grace of God and when we became more comfortable with our identities being in Christ, that is when our friendship truly deepened, and love—Jesus' love—covered a multitude of sins.

What has become the center of your life in your local church?

QUESTIONS

In what areas are you exhibiting spiritual pride and spiritual covetousness? Spend some time thinking through this issue. Do you see this in any people around you? If so, how can you address this with Christian love and humility, taking heed lest you fall?

What issue(s) have you raised to be high water marks of sanctification? How do you approach issues in life that are not necessarily in black and white in Scripture? Can you discern between sin and secondary issues? What methods do you use when faced with a challenging situation? Where does the gospel come into play in all this?

PRAYER

Most merciful Lord, lift the veil that hinders my sight. Reveal my hidden faults. "Keep back your servant also from presumptuous sins; let them not have dominion over me!" Come Holy Spirit, convict me and my brothers and sisters in church of where we have walked away from the gospel. Work in our midst to turn our hearts back to Christ. Give us the blessing of being fruitful servants. Teach us how to be charitable with one another over issues that are not of primary importance. Bring us to one-mind on issues of first-importance. Bless us with unity, charity, and peace with the brethren. "Let the words of my mouth and the meditation of my heart be acceptable in your sight, O Lord, my rock and my redeemer." Amen.

CHAPTER FOUR:

Missional Gospel Amnesia

What has become the center of your missional activity?

THE DIMUNITION OF MISSIONS: A SYMPTOM OF GOSPEL AMNESIA

Have you ever believed, falsely, that evangelism and missions distract from discipling your own children?

Almost three years ago some friends of mine brought up the fact that my heart and my efforts in the church were far removed from evangelism and missions, and that it ought not be so. I denied that there was anything wrong, sulked, and even threw tantrums back at home. What's all the fuss you may wonder? Ah, wait till you see how tricky Satan can be, using gospel amnesia to demonize disciple making, evangelism and desire for the nations to know and glorify God. He took each one of these three Great Commission imperatives and twisted them in my mind so that I actually objected to them as ways of taking spiritual food out of our children's mouths. We were so obsessed over raising godly children that we saw evangelism and missions as a sideline issue at best and more as a diversion than anything else. Gospel amnesia made my heart cold and uncaring toward all unbelievers, known or unknown. This explains why the concept of Christian mission was so easy to disregard, either as something for the professionals (who *obviously* didn't care about sacrificing *their* children for the sake of unbelievers), or in a semi-hypercalvinistic way: *God is fully sovereign, so why bother evangelizing?*

Furthermore, under the full control of gospel amnesia, any whiff of evangelism and missionary outreach smelled of being "seeker sensitive," "program driven," and neglecting our own children and pew-mates to go disciple the unbeliever, which would be wasted effort because after all, they were *unbelievers*. I shake my head while writing this. It is shameful to admit, but how else does one bring out the deeds of darkness into the light.

It's taken a very long time for me to understand and internalize that being a "missional" Christian does not necessarily mean we stand at street corners or go door to door evangelizing, nor does it entail going on a missions trip, or simply giving more money for *other* people to go on missions trips. Although any of those things can be part of someone who is mission minded and missions gifted. A few summers ago, I remember for the first time encountering John Piper's words: "Missions is not the ultimate goal of the church. Worship is. Missions exists because worship doesn't. Worship is ultimate, not missions, because God is ultimate, not man."[26] In my still partially gospel amnesic mind I felt relieved, but also vindicated. I

---

[26] John Piper, *Let The Nations Be Glad*, John Piper (Michigan: Baker Academic, 2010), 35

didn't really stop to think about what he said; I just kept thinking to myself "Ha! Even John Piper says missions is not important and he's somebody who is all into Jesus!" I groan at my idiotic blindness right now as I write this. (I should have added long before now that a side-effect of gospel amnesia in someone like me is stupidity.) That Piper quote, I later found out, is the first few lines of his book, *Let The Nations Be Glad!* That quote goes on: "When this age is over, and the countless millions of the redeemed fall on their faces before the throne of God, missions will be no more. It is a temporary necessity. But worship abides forever."[27] Not only is Piper providing an important corrective to faddish approaches to missions work, but he is also pointing us to the eschaton, which is something all of us would do well to keep in mind. I also deeply appreciate Piper's reference to the words of John Stott, which have helped bring Christ back to the center of my thinking in this area:

> The highest of missionary motives is neither obedience to the Great Commission (important as that is), nor love for sinners who are alienated and perishing (strong as that incentive is, especially when we contemplate the wrath of God...), but rather zeal—burning and passionate zeal—for the glory of Jesus Christ... Only one imperialism is Christian... and that is concern for His Imperial Majesty Jesus Christ, and for the glory of his

---

[27] John Piper, *Let The Nations Be Glad*, John Piper (Michigan: Baker Academic, 2010), 35

empire.[28]

Being a missional Christian is being a Christian who loves Jesus and has been so transformed by that love that you desire it intensely for all those that God brings your way. Let us not allow, as I did for so long, the word "missional" to become a distraction, some mere buzzword that is in vogue today in certain parts of the Church.[29] The idea goes back to the dominion mandate in Genesis 1:28. The goal is to press forward the glory of God in all the earth. As I am transformed into the image of God from one degree of glory to another I am discipling as I go, I am worshiping and calling others to worship God. The goal is worship. I don't know how others define it, but this is my working definition.

In my library I have a copy of *Good News For Modern Man, The New Testament: Today's English Version* Bible, which an American missionary in Greece gave to my father when he was a recent émigré from Iraq. On the inside flap he wrote:

> To Issam, To help you remember the day when you asked Jesus Christ to enter your heart... and to help you <u>grow</u> in your new personal relationship with

---

[28] John Piper, *Let The Nations Be Glad,* John Piper quoting John Stott, ellipses by Piper (Michigan: Baker Academic, 2010) 10

[29] We should have no problem in principle with trendy buzzwords in Christian circles coming in and out of favor. God has used them at least as far back as Christians were called "The Way." (Acts 9:2) If it helps at all, realize that the word "evangelical" no longer means "fervent about spreading the good news to the world;" today it is primarily used to mean "believing Christian," or possibly "Protestant." We need a word to replace what evangelical meant just a few decades ago. "Missional" appears to fit the bill.

Him.

– With love and prayer, R... P....

It was signed on Friday January 20, 1978. My dad, Issam, made a confession of faith on the train from Athens to Thessaloniki after taking my nana (his mother) to the airport as she flew back to Iraq, the home of my heritage. That was the last time my father saw my grandmother. We immigrated to America in December of that year.

I, of all people, given my history, should have displayed a tenderness and a softness in the area of missions and evangelism. I am grateful for the man who evangelized my father. If he had not left America to go to Greece where he crossed paths with my father, I don't know where or who I would be right now. My salvation, my Christian marriage and the salvation of my children are directly traceable to that man who had been a faithful follower of Christ, that man who was willing to go to the nations and talk to all the people the Lord sent his way about the glorious gospel of Jesus Christ.[30]

I cry every time I open my dad's old Bible, which I do a few times a year now to remind myself of the grace of God, and the importance of missionary work. It was

---

[30] To clarify: I know that if God wanted to redeem me, he would have used *someone* to call us to Christ even if *this* man had not been faithful. The Lord accomplishes all his holy will; nothing thwarts him. Still, I am awe-struck at the significant consequences of one man's obedience

later in 1978, sitting in the train station in Thessaloniki, that my father spoke the gospel to me. I believed and confessed that Jesus Christ died for my sins on the cross. I was eight years old.

When I was nineteen and still living with my parents I started attending a church that had a strong emphasis on international missions, that encouraged participating in such travels, and I became interested in such missions along with the predominant culture within that church. Although I had been in America since I was nine, my sister and I were raised in a traditional Iraqi home. Young single girls don't just leave their parents' home to become missionaries. Without the prospect of personal involvement in an international trip, I buried my interest in missions, and I moved on with my life.

A lot of years have passed by since then, a lot of years spent with an aversion to missions and distaste toward evangelism. But my God is faithful; my Lord saves to the uttermost. I find that he is restoring the years that the locusts ate. I now have very dear friendships with missionaries in both the Middle East and Africa, and I am finding ways to express my passion for missions even without lacing up my sandals, so to speak. I have found that the words of Pastor John Piper and Pastor David Platt have repeatedly helped transform my mind and heart completely toward missions.

THE DIMINUTION OF EVANGELISM: A SYMPTOM OF GOSPEL AMNESIA

Objectively, we all know that not everyone is called to be a missionary or professional evangelist. But all Christians are called to desire the glory of God above all things and one of the ways God is glorified is through faithfulness to the Great Commission.

When we have gospel amnesia, *and* we are operating from a weak or maybe a hazy understanding of the atoning work of Christ, it doesn't take long before evangelism drops off the radar. There was a time my husband and I firmly held that our responsibility for evangelism extended to our children's spiritual welfare *only*. Otherwise it was the calling of the select few whom God gifted specifically to evangelize. We eschewed evangelism in favor of proselytizing others into our way of thinking about faith, church, and family. This really hit home with me when I read Jonathan Dodson's *Unbelievable Gospel*.

Dodson sets up this convicting contrast:

> "Proselytizing is motivated by recruitment. Those who proselytize try to recruit people to different things... The proselytizer puts faith in rational arguments and in social networks. *Whatever is of greatest value to us motivates our proselytizing.* Depending on your values, Christianity may have its strongest expression in a political party, a moral code, a view of the book of Revelation, form or denomination of church, or doctrinal stance. *Notice*

> *that none of these are focused on Jesus. We all recruit to what we think is most important.* Men recruit to sports teams; women recruit to fashion trends. In the case of the proselytizer, he recruits to faith in a messiah and lord other than Jesus. On the whole, faith is placed in the messiah of church and the lord of doctrine. *This false gospel goes something like: 'If you join the right church and get the right doctrine, then you can be saved.' The true gospel simply says: 'If you join Jesus through repentance and faith, then he will save you.'* Quite different."[31] (Emphasis mine)

This paragraph, especially the parts that I emphasized, pierced the heart of a recovering gospel amnesiac like myself and drove deep the sad knowledge that I had abandoned the supremacy and excellencies of Christ for drivel. Because everything compared to Christ is drivel. The Apostle Paul in Philippians 3:8 says:

> Indeed, I count everything as loss because of the surpassing worth of knowing Christ Jesus my Lord. For his sake I have suffered the loss of all things and count them as rubbish, in order that I may gain Christ. —Philippians 3:8

Our thoughts and actions belied our spoken orthodox faith statements those years. What we were actually saying was that living and worshiping in a particular

---

[31] Jonathan Dodson, *Unbelievable Gospel: How to Share a Gospel Worth Believing* (GCD Press, 2012)

way as Christians, was *more important* than the Son of God and his gospel.

Evangelism within the borders of the North American continent as well as the rest of the world is absolutely critical as we see more clearly the affects of a post-Christian culture. For those of us that care deeply about the unborn babies being sacrificed every day, boys and girls sold into sex slavery, baby girls left to die because of their gender, abuse, rape, hunger, war, crime, and a host of other affects of the ravages of sin on this world, *we cannot afford the cost of gospel amnesia.* We cannot afford it in ourselves and we cannot sit around while our brothers and sisters in Christ are off on tangents while the culture around us mocks and blasphemes the name of Jesus because of our anemic testimony. We cannot in good conscience as Christians live for the peace and well being (physical *or* spiritual) of ourselves and our children while neglecting Christ's specific calling to pick up our crosses and live for the sake of his *name.*

What has become the center of your missional activity?

QUESTIONS

Do you care that there are people all around the world, near and far, who have not heard about Jesus? If so, what part can you play in the plan of God, who desires his gospel to go to all the nations?

Do you have a heart for people in countries and cultures

that have a Christian history and cultural remnants, but where confessional Christianity is in decline? Do you tend to think of their situation more politically or missionally?

Do you have friends or neighbors who don't know Christ? How would you describe your heart attitude toward them? How would you describe your speech and actions toward them? When you meditate on the gospel, does it make you want to share it with others?

PRAYER

Holy Father, soften my heart toward my fellow man. Give me tenderness for the widow, the orphan, the weak, and the outcast. Teach me how to live within a discipleship mindset. Help me to give cheerfully and abundantly to missions endeavors, as you lead. May the name of Jesus be glorified and worshiped to the ends of the earth. Amen.

CHAPTER FIVE:

Denominational Gospel Amnesia

What is at the center for you in your denominational tradition?

There was a time, when I remember being unwilling to fellowship with, read books by, or listen to sermons of anyone who I believed did not subscribe to most, if not all the church-related issues to which I had attached myself. This included some pretty esoteric theological minutiae. It wasn't enough for me that they held the gospel dearly, or even held to Reformed doctrine. They also had to hold to all the secondary and tertiary issues I had raised to primary importance. Anyone who was "all about Jesus" was quickly dismissed as either, immature and superficial, and/or most likely "seeker sensitive." My arrogance was absolutely astounding. For the sake of full disclosure, during those years (with the exception of reading *Desiring God* early on before the blindness had completely set in) I would not listen to men like John Piper, Don Carson, or Tim Keller, men with whom I knew each differed from me theologically in at least one way. In his gracious and merciful providence, God *drove* me to the teaching of these men over the last several years as he used them *mightily* (no exaggeration) to draw me and my husband out of the darkness of gospel amnesia. These men have become fathers in the faith to me. It is no idolatry to give honor where honor is due (Rom. 13:7).

Unfortunately, I am not alone in mocking and disdaining un-like-minded denominations. Many partake of this rancid feast with each other in public and in private.

By sectarian gospel amnesia I am addressing the tendency of one sect of Christians to marginalize, scoff, scorn, caricature, or actively abuse another sect. The following quote from Tim Keller in *The Reason for God*, crystalized my thoughts regarding sectarian gospel amnesia.

> It is widely believed that one of the main barriers to world peace is religion, and especially the major traditional religions with their exclusive claims to superiority. It may surprise you that though I am a Christian minister I agree with this. Religion, generally speaking, tends to create a slippery slope in the heart. Each religion informs its followers that they have "the truth," and this naturally *leads them to feel superior to those with differing beliefs*. Also, a religion tells its followers that they are saved and connected to God by devotedly performing that truth. *This moves them to separate from those who are less devoted and pure in life. Therefore, it is easy for one religious group to stereotype and caricature other ones. Once this situation exists it can easily spiral down into the marginalization of others or even to active oppression, abuse, or*

violence against them.[32] (Emphases mine)

Sadly, I believe these words are just as applicable to Trinitarian Christian sects and their interactions with each other. Whether we are Catholics, Presbyterians, Baptists, Lutherans, Methodists, Orthodox, or "non-denominational" (and all the micro-denominations birthed since the Reformation) we have to ask: What has become the center for our sect/denomination? Even those under the non-denominational banner partake in reviling and scorning. This is not limited to the Western Church.

I understand we live in a fallen world and one of the consequences of our limited and finite understanding of the Word of God is doctrinal differences. I think of Peter and Paul, of Paul and Mark, Catholics versus the Protestant Reformers, the Puritans, etc. Starting with Luther and Zwingli at the Marburg Colloquy (1529), Protestantism has been plagued with division, not merely diversity. My aim is not to minimize doctrinal convictions and push for ecumenicalism at all costs. Not at all! I have my own theological convictions, which I have arrived at through much struggle and study, and I have reasons to believe what I believe. However, my humble plea is for charity in line with the gospel, especially toward those in the household of God. Keeping the gospel at center helps us to remember that the gospel is universal. "There is <u>one</u> Lord, <u>one</u> faith, <u>one</u> baptism, <u>one</u> God and Father of all, who is over all

---

[32] Timothy Keller, *The Reason for God: Belief in an Age of Skepticism* (New York: Riverhead Books, 2008), 4–5

and through all and in all" (Eph. 4:5–6)

TRADITIONALISM: A SYMPTOM OF GOSPEL AMNESIA

There is nothing wrong with denominational traditions. Just like there is nothing wrong with denominational doctrine. But *traditionalism* can be just as much an idol as power, sex, or money. "Tradition is the living faith of the dead; traditionalism is the dead faith of the living."[33] Whether it is the grievous killing between Protestants and Catholics of centuries past, or shunning of one group of Christians by another and every other shameful warring over tradition within the Body of Christ, at the heart, is gospel amnesia—we have forgotten the gospel.

To be clear: corruption, heresy, abuse, legalistic or liberal teachings and wolvery are to be contended with the full weight of the gospel and the sheep protected. We do not wink at things that bring blasphemy upon the name of Christ. However, much of what I see as I look out onto the Evangelical landscape is a zeal for what I have labeled traditionalism.

Traditionalism is an inordinate attachment to ones traditions. Here is Jesus' view on traditionalism:

> And he said to them, "Well did Isaiah prophesy of you hypocrites, as it is written, "'This people honors me with their lips, but their heart is far from me; in

---

[33] Jaroslav Pelikan, *The Vindication of Tradition* (New Haven: Yale University Press, 1986) 65

vain do they worship me, teaching as doctrines the commandments of men.' You leave the commandment of God and hold to the tradition of men." And he said to them, "You have a fine way of rejecting the commandment of God in order to establish your tradition! [...T]hus making void the word of God by your tradition that you have handed down. And many such things you do."—Mark 7:6—8,13

This response from Jesus came after the Pharisees were complaining to him about his disciples not washing their hands before eating. Our traditions may or may not fall under the ceremonial rubric like the Jewish washing traditions.[34] They can be anything from "this is how we've always done it at this church" to paraments or banners and vestments or robes. Every church has traditions, just like every church has a liturgy whether the church uses these terms or not. Although traditions are not wrong *per se,* if they are unhinged from the gospel, they will degenerate into traditionalism. When these types of things move to the center and displace the gospel, the organization has "wittingly or unwittingly"[35] marginalized Christ.

I have probably spent more years of my life observing Lent than not. Sometimes out of tradition, sometimes

---

[34] Even if our traditions have a common sense origin, like washing hands before eating, neglecting to do so never deserves a rebuke on *religious* grounds in Christian circles.

[35] Andrew David Naselli, "*D.A. Carson's Theological Method,*" *Scottish Bulletin of Evangelical Theology* (2011): 248–249 (Emphases in the original)

out of conviction, sometimes out of humility, and sometimes out of arrogance, pride and moral-superiority. I've done it as a Chaldean Catholic; I've done it as a Syriac Orthodox; I've done it as a Lutheran, and I've done it as a Reformed Presbyterian, both in church bodies that corporately observed, and those which corporately ignored this part of the church calendar. We have observed Lent privately as a family, and corporately with our church body. We even "observed" it one year in our home by self-consciously and vocally "giving up Lent" for Lent. Honestly, I'm having difficulty thinking of any time in which I didn't approach this season with some kind of baggage.

My point here isn't whether or not we should all start observing the season of Lent. My point is to drive home what traditionalism can do to a Christian—usurp the place of Christ in the heart and plunge us into gospel amnesia. I know you may find this example very peculiar since Lent is a season of mourning, fasting and repentance of sin—which should after all be reminding us of Jesus. Yet, even in such beautiful symbol–laden activity we can find ourselves distracted away (Distraction Mode) from the person and cross work of Jesus Christ.

I am not pushing for an abandonment of distinctives, church traditions and the like. And I certainly don't think that we should let the fear of traditionalism cause us to abandon traditions. Living with the gospel at center means we can ask God to breathe new life (if it be his will) into a dying/dead tradition—reclaiming/

redeeming it by faith! It is, however, an area where we have to be vigilant, there is a "danger to absolutizing and enforcing any tradition."[36] In Galatians 2: 11–14 we see Peter acting out of fear and hypocrisy as he reverted back to the Jewish laws of refusing table fellowship with the uncircumcised. This was a pivotal moment in the life of the early church. Peter was an *Apostle* who was *falsifying the gospel* at the level of church culture, albeit not doctrinally.[37] This was so serious that we read in Gal. 2:11 of Paul rebuking him to his face publicly for living out-of-line with the truth of the gospel (Gal. 2:14). So although he was not rejecting the gospel theologically his actions spoke lies about what he believed. Gospel doctrine and gospel action go together! In this passage we see that the gospel was at stake because of Peter's actions—his gospel amnesia. In all these things, we must find ways to stay tethered to the gospel. If we find that a tradition cannot be practiced without serious compromise to the gospel or usurpation of Christ in the heart, then a lot of prayer and reflection is in order.

The Lord has used the gospel to remove some of the barnacles off our family traditions. Our desire is to model for our children parents who are humbly submitting all for the sake of Jesus Christ.

---

[36] Ray Ortlund Jr., "Justification versus Self–Justification," (Paper presented at The Gospel Coalition National Conference, April 13, 2011)

[37] Ibid

LACK OF LOVE FOR ONE ANOTHER: A SYMPTOM OF GOSPEL AMNESIA

At first glance, this section may seem redundant to the reader. I wrote specifically about Christian charity in chapter three while here I address love within the Body: inter- and intra-denominational. Within the context of Romans 14 and secondary issues, kindness and tolerance toward our fellow brethren is a mark of gospel living. Such charity and tolerance can be considered *passive*, whereas the John 13:35 love described in this section is more *active* in nature.

> By this all people will know that you are my disciples, if you have love for one another.—John 13:35

This is not a cute Sunday school lesson or a child's ditty, this is the commandment of Jesus. Love like this, is *the* mark of Christianity. It is this love that distinguishes (or should distinguish) us from the other religions and the culture around us. I am not so sure, as I look out across the Christian landscape with it's factions, schisms, and internet fights, if the Lord is seeing the kind of love the gospel calls forth from believers. And because I believe a lack of love within the Body stems from forgetting the gospel, I want to exhort all of us, together. We read in 1 John:

> Whoever says he is in the light and hates his brother is still in darkness, Whoever loves his brother abides in the light, and in him there is no cause for

stumbling. But whoever hates his brother is in the darkness and walks in the darkness, and does not know where he is going, because the darkness has blinded his eyes. 1 John 2:9–11

See what kind of love the Father has given to us, that we should be called children of God; and so we are. 1 John 3:1

For this is the message that you have heard from the beginning, that we should love one another. We should not be like Cain, who was of the evil one and murdered his brother. And why did he murder him? Because his own deeds were evil and his brother's righteous.... We know that we have passed out of death into life, because we love the brothers. Whoever does not love abides in death. Everyone who hates his brother is a murderer, and you know that no murderer has eternal life abiding in him. By this we know love, that he laid down his life for us, and we ought to lay down our lives for the brothers. 1 John 3:11–16

Beloved, let us love one another, for love is from God, and whoever loves has been born of God and knows God. Anyone who does not love does not know God, because God is love. In this the love of God has made manifest among us, that God sent his only Son into the world, so that we might live through him. In this is love, not that we have loved God but that he loved us and sent his Son to be the

> propitiation for our sins. Beloved, if God so loved us, we also ought to love one another. No one has ever seen God; if we love one another, God abides in us and his love is perfected in us. 1 John 4:7–12
>
> If anyone says, "I love God," and hates his brother, he is a liar; for he who does not love his brother whom he has seen cannot love God whom he has not seen. And this commandment we have from him: whoever loves God must also love his brother. 1 John 4:20–21

Given what the Word of God says above, regarding loving the brethren, what type of people ought we to be with those inside our traditions and without? I have been a person that has hated, murdered in the heart, and broken all the directives of the above verses. It was the day that I saw that ugliness, sitting on my couch shaking from the unveiling of my heart that I realized the gravity and darkness of gospel amnesia. And I knew, that I didn't want to ever forget or discount the gospel again.

Of course, I have gone on to sin again with a broken and imperfect love. (I am still a fallen woman.) The reason I don't love people the way Christ has commanded me to, is because I still struggle to believe the gospel in my heart. We don't love because we have gospel amnesia, either episodically or chronically.

The love to which God calls us is not necessarily a feeling but actions empowered by the gospel to speak to and treat our brethren with charity. In Philippians 2:1–2 Paul exhorts the believers in this way, "So if there is any encouragement in Christ, any comfort from love, any participation in the Spirit, any affection and sympathy, complete my joy by being of the same mind, having the same love, being in full accord and of one mind." Paul says this knowing that in all the churches he had planted there were people given diverse gifts by the Spirit, they may have been of different opinions on a variety of issues, plus there were the Jew and Gentile relationships. The exhortation is *not* to be identical, but to be of one mind in Christ seeking the glorify of God in all things. This "like-mindedness" does not necessarily mean that we have to be of the same opinions on non-central issues. The call to love is driven by the gospel and focused on Christ, not on whether we agree with each other on every jot and tittle. Thus, intra and inter-denominational love can exist within the Body of Christ, if Christ stays at the center.

What is at the center for you in your denominational tradition?

QUESTIONS

Which church or denominational traditions have you attached your heart to? Do you become angry when you perceive someone desiring a change in those traditions? List some ways you can work, with grace and humility, with someone who sets a different value on those traditions.

Do you have friends from other denominational traditions? If so, what is your response when they disagree with you on doctrine or church traditions?

What is your response to an article on a Christian website which you disagree with? How can you disagree in line with John 13:35? Is your disagreement laced with scoffing and mockery?

Many people today justify a use of "Christian" mockery, defending their argument on the fact that Elijah did it. Is this in line with John 13:35? Is this in line with the law of Christ?

What is your response or the response of those in your circles to someone inside or outside your group who is objectively in the wrong (doctrinally, or otherwise)? When contending for the faith with those who are objectively wrong, do you use tactics such as degrading or harsh speech? How can you be firm in your stance, but carry yourself with humility and love in line with John 13:35?

PRAYER

Most merciful Father, I confess to you that there is much hostility in my heart toward my brethren. Free me from this. Take away my gospel amnesia in this area. Through your Holy Spirit pour into me a John 13:35 love for the brethren. Shake me out of my traditionalism. Free me from the bondage that believes I am always right. Forgive me for not holding my views with grace and humility. Forgive me for combative words and actions. Through your grace and mercy help me to live at peace with all men. Kill the sins of scoffing, mockery, and the idolization of satire in my heart. Those are the ways of a fool, Father, I desire to be made into the image of Christ in this area and not a fool. Will you grant this prayer in the strong name of Jesus,

Amen.

CHAPTER SIX:

Cultural Gospel Amnesia

What is at the center of our Church culture as the Body of Christ?

We can see how gospel amnesia can build up starting from the personal level, layer upon layer, until we get to its effects on the entire culture around us. We often hear that the Church as a whole has lost cultural influence over the last several centuries. An alternative way to look at this trend is that the *culture* (which in the West was once saturated with Christian thought) has *forgotten* about the gospel, giving less and less mindshare to Christ and his Church. The difference in these two perspectives is whether the Church is perceived to be acting (or failing to act) *on* culture or *in* culture. If we continue to believe that the Church acts *on* culture, we can push the responsibility onto that corporate entity, "the Church," and forget that we, as individual Christians, are *acting in the culture with everything we do*.[38]

There are two ways the Church loses its saltiness and its position within the surrounding culture: One, when the Church in its preaching and practices looks no different

---

[38] I recommend D.A. Carson's *Christ & Culture Revisited* for a balanced treatment of the relationship of the church to culture.

then the world (e.g. teaching is reduced to self-help guidelines, "how to be a better you" culture, peace- and prosperity-oriented). Two, when the Church retreats into a corner, refusing to engage culture. In both of these cases the image of the gospel presented to the world is anemic and lies about who God is and what he has done in Christ.

In my own life, I took the second route. I tried defending my retreat and my seeking out of an exclusively like-minded Christian subculture by calling it an "advance by retreat." That is, I claimed God's call in the Old Testament for Israel to separate from the nations as a calling that stands for today's Christians.[39] I saw the parts of the church that were living no differently form the world and in my gospel amnesia I was quick to judge, and quick to err in the other direction.

GOSPEL AMNESIA: LIVING NO DIFFERENTLY THAN THE WORLD

Josiah became king of Jerusalem when he was eight years old and reigned for thirty-one years. He purged the land from idolatry, broke down altars, cut down images, killed the priests of the false gods and cleansed all of Israel (including the northern region) from apostasy and idol worship. He sought to restore the temple and the rightful worship of God. The people had *forgotten* the law of God and polluted the temple

---

[39] The role of Israel in the Old Testament and how it relates to New Testament believers is an important theological point lying outside the scope of the current discussion.

through syncretism. In the eighteenth year of his reign, he had the priests purify and repair the temple. Let's look to see what this portion of Scripture says to us regarding gospel amnesia:

> While they were bringing out the money that had been brought into the house of the Lord, Hilkiah the priest found the Book of the Law of the Lord given through Moses. Then Hilkiah answered and said to Shaphan the secretary, 'I have found the Book of the Law in the house of the Lord.' and Hilkiah gave the book to Shaphan. Shaphan brought the book to the king... And Shaphan read from it before the king. *And when the king heard the words of the Law, he tore his clothes.* And the king commanded Hilkiah, Ahikam the son of Shaphan, Abdon the son of Micah, Shaphan the secretary, and Asaiah the king's servant, saying, 'Go inquire of the Lord for me and for those who are left in Israel and in Judah, concerning the words of the book that has been found. For great is the wrath of the Lord that is poured out on us, because our fathers have not kept the word of the Lord, to do according to all that is written in this book. (Emphasis mine) 2 Chronicles 34:14–16,18–21

This story is one display of gospel amnesia; revealing the consequences of forgetting the words of God, and waking up to how far off base they were. Their gospel amnesia was so extensive that Josiah tears his clothes (a symbol of ruin, grief, sorrow and distress) at hearing the Word of God. Think Distraction Mode, although in this case it's not distraction with good things but with the things of the world. Israel at the time was deep into syncretism with the surrounding cultures.

When the people forgot the words of their God, they fell into all manner of sin, this affected their surrounding culture. It is the same for us when we forget or minimize Jesus Christ. Many Christians today have forgotten the law of Christ (Gal. 6:2). The gospel which should be on our minds, in our hearts, on our lips, and lived out before a watching world, is either forgotten because of distraction with the things of this world, resulting in compromise, worldliness or syncretism; or because of a focus on "righteous living," or traditionalism that goes so far as to become a distraction. Either way, *the results are the same* and they have an affect on the culture in which we live, on unbelievers in our lives, fellow brothers and sisters in Christ, and on the "back-slidden" Christian.

If we are distracted by the things of the world and fall into gospel amnesia, then we will neither speak nor live any differently than the unbeliever. Why would an unbeliever or back-slidden Christian turn to Christ if our witness says, "Christ cannot transform?" Thus, we neglect to bring the hope and mercy of Christ to our neighbors, including our spouses and children (our nearest neighbors). Moreover, when we forget or domesticate the gospel we become like the seed that fell on rocky ground, or those among thorns. We will not be able to withstand the onslaught of tribulation or persecutions and the relentlessness of the cares of this world.

If 'righteous living' becomes a distraction which diminishes the gospel, then we will be wrapped up in ourselves, becoming so self-focused that we are impotent as vessels for the work of Christ in this culture. Actually, it doesn't just make us practically ineffectual, it subverts the real work of the gospel in us. This happens because our righteous living becomes an idol and all such idols vie for the place of god in our souls.

We live no differently from the world in that while we may have a different morality, we have the same motives (e.g. self) use the same tools (e.g. politics) and suffer the same despair, and plot the same vengeance when we don't get our way.

We see the effect of gospel amnesia all around us, it's just that we haven't thought of it or labeled it this way. For example, we have a culture that is increasingly hostile to Christians, and although we can claim that Christ said the world will reject us, this is not the only reason Western culture is turning against Christianity at this time. We should *long* for the time when the world rejects us for the *right* reasons, but unfortunately we give them plenty of unbiblical reasons to reject us now. The culture outside the Church wouldn't be so quick to label Christians as "haters" if they knew and identified Christians with the gospel, instead of with moralistic political charlatans, and Christians wouldn't be so shamed and flat-footed in responding to that accusation if we hadn't forgotten the gospel ourselves.

GOSPEL AMNESIA: RETREATING INTO A CHRISTIAN SUBCULTURE

Those of us in conservative Christian circles have heard a lot of talk on 'worldliness,' 'worldly Christians,' 'the world in the Church,' 'worldly youth groups,' and so on. Worldliness is a real biblical category, but through repetition and dilution it has not only become Christian jargon but has become the "sink" into which we want to throw out all our garbage. We tend to want to blame everything on wordiness, with the assumption that it is something that is only out there, outside of us.

Setting aside the Christianese let's explore some Scripture:

> Do not love the *world* or the things in the *world*. If anyone loves the *world*, the love of the Father is not in him. For all that is in the *world*—the desires of the flesh and the desires of the eyes and pride in possessions—is not from the Father but is from the *world*. And the *world* is passing away along with its desires, but whoever does the will of God abides forever. 1 John 2:15–17 (Emphases mine)

and,

> You adulterous people! Do you not know that friendship with the *world* is enmity with God? Therefore whoever wishes to be a friend of the

> *world* makes himself an enemy of God. Or do you suppose it is to no purpose that the Scripture says, 'He yearns jealously over the spirit that he has made to dwell in us.' James 4:4–5 (Emphases mine)

So the Lord takes worldliness seriously, and condemns it strongly. But then Scripture also says:

> For God so loved the *world*, that he gave his only Son, that whoever believes in him should not perish but have eternal life. For God did not send his Son into the *world* to condemn the *world*, but in order that the *world* might be saved through him.... And this is the judgment: the light has come into the *world*, and people loved the darkness rather than the light because their works were evil. John 3:16–17,19 (Emphases mine)

> But now I am coming to you, and these things I speak in the *world*, that they may have my joy fulfilled in themselves. I have given them your word, and the *world* has hated them because they are not of the *world*, just as I am not of the *world*. I do not ask that you take them out of the *world*, but that you keep them from the evil one. They are not of the *world*, just as I am not of the *world*. Sanctify them in the truth; your word is truth. As you sent me into the *world*, so I have sent them into the *world*. And for their sake I consecrate myself, that they also may be sanctified in truth... The glory that you have given me I have given to them, that they may be one even as we are one, I in them and you in

me, that they may become perfectly one, so that the *world* may know that you sent me and loved them even as you loved me. John 17:13–19,22–23 (Emphases mine)

You are the light of the *world*. A city set on a hill cannot be hidden. Nor do people light a lamp and put it under a basket, but on a stand, and it gives light to all in the house. In the same way, let your light shine before others, so that they may see your good works and give glory to your Father who is in heaven. Matthew 5:14–16 (Emphases mine)

In the above verses, the word for *"world"* is the Greek word *kosmos*. In studying Scripture, context and storyline are of primary importance in determining meaning. The word *kosmos*—world—has a range of meaning and nuance in the Bible. There are places where "world" means planet earth. Other times "world" is referring to "the human race external to the Jewish nation, the heathen world,"[40] or, "the human race, emphasizing both Jew and Gentile."[41] Yet, in another definition, "world" is used to refer to the sinful state of man. D.A. Carson says that in John's Gospel, "world" "is this human–centered, created order that God has made and that has rebelled against him in hatefulness and

---

[40] *Mounce Concise Greek–English Dictionary of the New Testament*, electronic source: Accordance Bible Software, version 10.0.5, C. 2011, http://www.teknia.com/greek-dictionary

[41] I am grateful to my friend, Mike Munoz, (M.A., Religion, Reformed Theological Seminary) for discussions about the nuances of *kosmos* in the Greek text.

idolatry, resulting in broken relationships, infidelity, and wickedness."[42] Now, God knows what he is doing when He inspires Scripture, and He could have chosen to use different words if He wanted these concepts totally separated. However, He chose to use the same word, and while we interpret and affirm these distinctions, we should keep in mind that there is a common word, and some common thread behind them as well. The "world" that God hates, we should hate. The "world" that God loves, we should love. The fact that it's the same word in both cases means it *is* possible for us to overshoot or undershoot when targeting what "worldliness" means.

If we know that God himself says that creation is good, that he is out to save, that he loves the world, and died on a cross, but that he hates sin, has conquered the ruler of this world (Satan) and is in the process of cleansing us out of that sin… where do we draw the line in the "world?" What does this have to do with gospel amnesia?

Let's look again at 1 John 2:15–17, what is the "world" that we are not to love? The verses spell it out clearly, I believe. The things of the world we are to reject are: "the desires of the flesh and the desires of the eyes and the pride in possessions." Where do we encounter the desires of the flesh, the desires of the eyes, and the pride in possessions? Are they *out* there somewhere? Yes *and* No! They are *in* us! They are *our* sinful man,

---

[42] D. A. Carson *The God Who Is There* (Michigan: Baker Books, 2010), 140

which is part of the "world."⁴³ The "world" that we are to despise and reject is the sinful state inside of *us*. It is the "world" *within* people. This includes me. Wherever I go, whatever I do, whomever I do things with, this will follow me. That worldliness I am "tsk–tsking" about is inside of me. It may look different than someone else's worldliness—individual, corporate, or cultural—but this doesn't mean I can forget my own.

When we have gospel amnesia we can get all these things confused. Forgetting the gospel, the good news of what God has done through Christ Jesus, what he has overcome *in us*, makes us believe that sin is *only* "out there" in the world, on the streets, at the mall, in the grocery stores, in the youth group, in the public schools, in the Christian schools, on all those farms owned by big companies, in cows that are given hormones, and in every church that doesn't worship and believe every jot and tittle the same way we do. We may begin to think that we can till a little plot of sinlessness in ourselves apart from the world, and we are careful to not let it become soiled by the world. We may allow others into our lives, if they also have their own little bit of sinlessness and we try together to hold on to that and defend against "the world" outside.

However, in our concentration on the sin that is *out in the world*, which we may rightly and justifiably reject, we tend to neglect or *diminish* what Jesus says here:

---

[43] B.B. Warfield, *God's Immeasurable Love*, http://www.opc.org/nh.html?article_id=160

> It is not what goes into the mouth that defiles a person, but what comes out of the mouth; this defiles a person. Matthew 15:11

There are two consequences to gospel amnesia in this area. One is forgetting God's love; the other is forgetting how much God hates sin. In fact, one can lead to the other and feed off each other. When we forget the all-conquering love, compassion and longsuffering of God —the love God has for the world, yes, God's love for "all that is evil and noisome and disgusting"[44]—we can end up hating the world, giving up on it, and disdaining people. This enables Christians to withdraw into their own subculture creating a voluntary Christian ghetto.

Certainly one would think when we are in this state we at least remember a truth about how much God hates sin, right? It may seem our only focus is God's hatred of sin: how bad it is and how to stay away from it. But forgetting the gospel means we have forgotten the love of God. *By forgetting God's love we can easily slip into forgetting the depth of our own sin because we focus on what we see as the world's sin.* Jerry Bridges writes in *Respectable Sins*, "conservative evangelicals may have become so preoccupied with some of the major sins of society around us that we have lost sight of the need to deal with our own more 'refined' or subtle sins."[45]

---

[44] B.B. Warfield, *God's Immeasurable Love*, http://www.opc.org/nh.html?article_id=160

[45] Jerry Bridges, *Respectable Sins* (Colorado: NavPress, 2007), 9

We use improper weights and measures when we misapply the gospel. When we are not living self-consciously within the horizon of the gospel, consistently and deliberately dwelling on it and applying it to every day life, we start believing that our debt to the perfect and infinite creator and sovereign God of this universe is less for our "lighter" sins and more for others "heavier" sins.

This is the darkness that was in my own heart. The heart that so readily forgot that I was saved by the grace of Jesus Christ alone and so quickly embraced the things of this world (while denying that fact). We tend to collapse 'worldliness" to include the major sins of our surrounding culture: sex, addictions, and rebellion, while neglecting the fact that Jesus said "worldliness" is a heart issue. The fact is: the sinful things of this world are inside of every heart. *The sinful things of this world are all the ways that we do what is right in our own eyes.* For those of us with gospel amnesia we can even find ways to practice self-denial and adherence to external rules (and call it "hating worldliness") in a way that is merely "right in our own eyes."

If Jesus loves sinners (redeemed and would-be-redeemed) then we need to love sinners. If Jesus loves his creation, we need to love his creation—we need to love the world. God's love for the world, Warfield says, is a marvel because "it is able to prevail over the holy God's hatred and abhorrence of sin!" He goes on to say that it is not a love of complacency, but a "love of *benevolence* which would fain save us from our worldliness, fleshliness, and devilishness." Concerning John 3:16, Warfield says:

> The key to the passage lies, therefore, you see, in the significance of the term "world." It is not here a term of extension so much as a term of intensity. Its primary connotation is ethical, and the point of its employment is not to suggest that the world is so *big* that it takes a great deal of love to embrace it all, but that the world is so *bad* that it takes a great kind of love to love it at all, and much more to love it as God has loved it when he gave his Son for it.[46]

He goes on to say that the John 3:16 passage is intended "to arouse in our hearts a wondering sense of the marvel and the mystery of the love of God for the sinful world—conceived, here, not quantitatively but qualitatively as, in its very distinguishing characteristic, sinful."[47] D.A. Carson has said something similar:

> But the text says, 'God so loved the world'—this broken and fallen world. It is as if God is saying to the world, 'Morally speaking, you are the people of the crippled knees. You are the people of the moral bad breath. You are the people of the rampaging Genghis Khan personality. You are hateful and spiteful and murderous. And you know what? I love you anyway—not because you are lovable but because I am that kind of God.' That is why in the

---

[46] B.B. Warfield, *God's Immeasurable Love*, http://www.opc.org/nh.html?article_id=160

[47] Ibid

Bible, this side of Genesis 3 [the Fall], God's love is always marveled at. God's love is wonderful, surprising, in some ways not the way it ought to be.[48]

So what does all this mean for people with gospel amnesia or recovering amnesiacs? It means we cannot as the Body of Christ (individually or collectively) seek the "safety" of our Christian ghettos, the comfortableness of our subcultures where we huddle with "like-minded" people and continually hide our light under the basket. It means obey Jesus when he says to let our light shine before all men so that they glorify our Father in heaven when they see our good works. (Matthew 5:16). There is an implication here that we will be executing good works, this should crush any apprehension of syncretism and enculturation in our dealings with our surrounding culture. The term used often these days is *engagement*, and this requires wisdom, discernment and a heart centered on the cross, a heart willing to love. It also means that as we are continually washed by the gospel we will see that over time the transformative power of the gospel will indeed kill the power of the worldliness in our hearts.

What is at the center of our Church culture as the Body of Christ?

---

[48] D.A. Carson, *The God Who Is There: Finding Your Place in God's Story* (Michigan: Baker Books, 2010), 140-141

QUESTIONS

What does your life say about who God is and what he has done in Christ Jesus? Where in your life have you displayed a false or anemic gospel to those around you?

Which tempts you to forget the gospel: worldliness or righteous living? Given what you have read about gospel amnesia, do you see any signs or seeds of it in your heart and life?

What are your tendencies toward the surrounding culture? Do you tend to retract to "safe" communities? Are you tempted by your surrounding culture to compromise God's call to holiness?

PRAYER

Our Father and our God, renew your people. Send your Holy Spirit to enliven your Church on earth. Make us to be salt and light to the watching world. Keep us from bringing blasphemes against your name by our lax or repugnant Christianity. Make us to be a people who will understand your love, grace and forgiveness so that we may better reflect it to this generation. Keep us from compromise and keep us from withdrawing. Sanctify us in your truth, your word is truth. We plead the prayers of Christ for us. Amen.

CHAPTER SEVEN:

Overcoming Gospel Amnesia

Gospel amnesia is not new. Paul was astonished that the Galatians were so quickly turning away from the grace of Christ, from the gospel he had originally preached to them. Peter writes in 2 Peter 1 to those who had forgotten that they were cleansed from their former sins. His remedy: Remember the gospel! Paul's remedy for the Galatians: Remember the gospel! The writer of Hebrews tells his readers: "Therefore we must pay much closer attention to what we have heard, lest we drift away from it" (Hebrews 2:1). *Remembering the gospel is a Biblical imperative.*

BEHOLD WHAT MANNER OF LOVE

As someone who had functionally set aside the gospel for many many years, I can say that one of the sources of gospel amnesia is confusion about and misunderstanding of the love of God. For many years I saw it as beneath the dignity of Christ to say that he can love people *personally*. Therefore, I don't think we can fully heal from gospel amnesia *until* we internalize a better understanding of the love of God in Christ Jesus.

> Behold what manner of love the Father has bestowed on us, that we should be called children of God! —1John 3:1 (NKJ)

For this verse I chose to use the NKJ translation, for its use of the word "behold." There is something jolting, striking, about this word. It conveys something that requires savoring and meditation. The love of God is so unlike the things we are used to as sinful people that it requires awe, it requires thought, it requires a beholding, and it requires a converted heart and mind in order to even begin to understand it.

Many of us carry baggage when it comes to the word "love." Living in a fallen world, we have all been sinned against and we have all sinned against others in this area. In our father-hungry culture we have skewed ideas of fatherhood, which we carry into our relationship with God. Parents are human and they fail often in reflecting the love of the Father to their children. I admit that my husband and I have fallen in this area, especially with our harsh tones and chastisement of our children. There is definitely a deficiency for all of us concerning biblical love. Moreover, some folks have been abused in ways that have wounded their souls deeply.[49]

The gospel speaks of God's love, and that love is shown supremely by the death of Jesus Christ on the cross. "By this we know love, that he laid down his life for us, and we ought to lay down our lives for the brothers" 1John 3:16. To borrow a phrase from D.A. Carson, "the cross is the most unqualified display of God's love." That is, the cross is where God's love is most powerfully

---

[49] For physical, sexual, or spiritual abuse I recommend *Mending the Soul: Understanding and Healing Abuse* by Steven R. Tracy

demonstrated. There are many ways we forget the love of God, which can, for some of us, lead to gospel amnesia.

One of the ways we "forget" the love of God is when we presume upon God's love. That is, we take it for granted. Think Presumption Mode here. Instead of being enthralled by it, it starts fading into the background like old wallpaper. We know it's there but we don't see its beauty and intricacies any longer. Our eyes start "beholding" other things. I have come to believe that the only way to keep the love of God fresh before our eyes is to be people who dwell deeply in the gospel every day. We must take ourselves in hand and speak to ourselves, (as Martyn Lloyd–Jones has suggested) reminding ourselves of who God is, what he has done in the person of Christ, and who we are in relation to him.

OVERCOMING GOSPEL AMNESIA

How then, can we overcome gospel amnesia?

The first and most important step to overcoming gospel amnesia (no matter the mode—Distraction, Progression, or Presumption) as I have experienced it and as the Lord has convinced me of, is a steeping of mind, heart and soul into the cross work of Jesus Christ. This means getting ahold of solid preaching and writings of the cross and studying them while we immerse ourselves in studying the cross in the Scriptures. (See recommended reading list in the Appendix). Now when I say the cross work of Christ it does not mean we limit our reading and study to those small sections in the gospels to the time of Christ's death, although that is not a bad place to start. However, one of the ways of overcoming gospel amnesia and its symptoms is to kill this truncated vision we have of what Jesus did on the cross. What I am actually suggesting is a redemptive-historical study of the work of Jesus Christ.

This steeping should go *concurrently* with desperate prayer for spirit awakening. Acknowledging we can do nothing without the grace of God, we plead for a desire to seek the things of God, we plead for a desire to read his Word, and we plead for the Lord to fill us with his Holy Spirit. "If you then, who are evil, know how to give good gifts to your children, how much more will the heavenly Father give the Holy Spirit to those who ask him!" (Luke 11:13.) While at the throne of grace we confess that we are presumptuous, blind, and easily distracted by the desires of our heart. We then plead with God to show us the glory of Jesus. We beg for the Spirit of God to be poured out upon us in great measure, to open our eyes and soften our necks. We ask to see Jesus, we beg for the love of Jesus to be breathed into us because we know we cannot attain it by any doing. The key here is to bend the knee and come to the Father as children, because we *are* his children as 1John 3:1 says.

When the first and thickest blanket of gospel amnesia was lifted I remember thinking about Jesus, I remember reading *The Jesus Storybook Bible* all the way through in maybe one or two sittings. I remember being able to say his name again and glorying in it. I distinctly remember my vocabulary very quickly becoming cross and gospel oriented. I wanted to talk about him, sing about him, and read about him all the time. What I am going to suggest may sound simplistic, but is very powerful and it requires both humility and self-discipline: Read *The Jesus Storybook Bible* from cover to cover within a short period of time. Here is why this simple tool works so profoundly. (This is not a requirement, just a tool.) The Lord has worked through the author Sally-Lloyd Jones to write a children's storybook Bible in which every story speaks of Jesus. I pray you see the significance of this.

This beautiful children's book could be the beginning of resetting how we see the entirety of the Bible. It will show us how the center of the entire Bible is the person and work of Jesus Christ. The Bible is not primarily about us and how we should live, although people are important to God. The Bible is not primarily about God's covenants, although he uses the concept of covenant to teach us about himself.

The Bible is about our King, Jesus Christ and how he is restoring his kingdom, recreating the entire cosmos, to the praise and to the glory of the Father. The Bible is about who God is, what he has done, and who we are in relation to him: Thy Kingdom come, thy will be done, from the first page to the last. *Understanding that changes EVERYTHING*. After this little exercise, it would be fruitful for the soul to study the entire Bible with an eye out for Jesus from beginning to end.

Second, we must consistently stay Jesus centered, gospel-centric. This is not a buzz word. Jesus and gospel–centrality is not a fad. He is our Savior and Sovereign King. Jesus is our Redeemer from all enslavement. Over and over again in the New Testament we are told how critical it is to remember the gospel. When we stay gospel-centered, all the other things in our life will align themselves properly. One of the most important ways of staying gospel-centered is to be consistently exposed to Christ-centered expository teaching. Because there is so much good teaching online we can easily fool ourselves into thinking that that can be enough to sustain us either primarily or as a supplement to our local church's preaching if it fails to be gospel-centered. I can't stress enough the importance of being in a local church whose primary focus is the person and cross work of Jesus Christ—and not in name only, but in word and deed.

Finally, we must strive for a correct understanding of who God is, what Jesus the Son did, and how the love of the Father and the Son is conveyed to us through the Holy Spirit. When we begin to understand and accept that Jesus loves us, only then will we be able to love from a divinely changed heart. And only then will we have a deeper appreciation and understanding of the gospel, which will cause us to see our spiritual progression not as a "getting over" the gospel but as a maturation and growing *into* the gospel. My personal prayer is that the Lord will bestow upon me the desire and wherewithal to spend the rest of my life plumbing the depths of the gospel of Jesus Christ. "... that in everything he might be preeminent."

PERSONAL HEALING

My rescue from gospel amnesia is as vivid to me as this imagery in Ezekiel:

> And when I passed by you and saw you wallowing in your blood, I said to you in your blood. 'Live!" I said to you in your blood, 'Live!' I made you flourish like a plant of the field. And you grew up and became tall and arrived at full adornment. Your breasts were formed, and your hair had grown; yet you were naked and bare. When I passed by you again and saw you, behold, you were at the age for love, and I spread the corner of my garment over you and covered your nakedness; I made my vow to you and entered into a covenant with you, declared the Lord God, and you became mine. Then I bathed you with water and washed off your blood from you and anointed you with oil. I clothed you also with embroidered cloth and shod you with fine leather. I wrapped you in fine linen and covered you with silk. And I adorned you with ornaments and put bracelets on your wrists and a chain on your neck. And I put a ring on your nose and earrings in your ears and a beautiful crown on your head. Ezekiel 16:6–12

Although I am convinced that the bondage and blindness I was under for many years has been removed, the struggle for faith and the fight to keep my eyes focused on Christ is part of my every day life. A starving emaciated person may be relieved of their immediate need by a good feast, but ongoing sustenance is necessary if that malnourished individual desires healing and a life of health and energy. And so it has been for me. I have to eat from the Lord Jesus every day. Just like I cannot maintain a healthy life off of one or two meals every now and then, I cannot maintain a healthy spiritual life without gospel-reliance each and every day.

The war against gospel amnesia, whether sustained or episodic, is a relentless, everyday fight. Every day we have a million opportunities to forget the gospel, and so every day we fight against that temptation by being stubbornly immovable theologically—we must stay gospel-centered. We must! One day, as I was fighting to hold on to the gospel, a friend emailed this to me:

> When the avenger of blood follows you, flee immediately to this sanctuary. Think: Let me not deny myself comfort and God glory both at once. 'Where sin abounds, grace abounds much more' (Rom. 5:20). Though sins after conversion stain our profession more than sins before conversion, go still to the glorious mercy of God. To seventy times seventy times, there is yet mercy. We beseech you be reconciled, said St. Paul to the Corinthians, when they were in the state of grace and already had their pardon. Let us never be

discouraged from going to Christ.[50]

Grace is a tireless hunter, chasing and overpowering me every day. It will not let me pay it back or earn my keep. The only appeasement it abides is complete surrender in quiet humility. Each day the Spirit harnesses me with grace. He is alive and powerful and palpable in inexpressible ways, always bringing me to the grace of Jesus:

> Do you wonder why the grace of God has found such enemies as it always has, especially in religions in which works are mingled with grace? It is because the contrary heart of man, being in a frame of enmity to God, sets itself most against that which God will be glorified in. Therefore we should labour to vindicate nothing so much as grace.... Let us vindicate that upon all occasions. For we live by grace, and we must die by grace and stand at the day of judgement by grace—not in our own righteousness, but in the righteousness of Christ, being found in him.[51]

What we as a family try to do to protect ourselves against the temptations of Presumption, Distraction, and Progression is not necessarily a "to do" list for

---

[50] Grateful to my friend Gloria Furman for encouraging me with Sibbes: *Glorious Freedom*, Richard Sibbes (The Banner Of Truth Trust, 1639, 2000), 81

[51] Richard Sibbes, *Glorious Freedom*, (The Banner Of Truth Trust, 1639, 2000), 74

overcoming gospel amnesia. After all, *that* is part of the problem. It's not that we don't *do* anything, it's that we do not *think about* Christianity in terms of *doing* but as *what Jesus has done and will do.* Our lives, our children and our spiritual health is no longer the focus, Jesus is. This is the reason I have stressed over and over again a gospel-centered theology. It has been our protection against Presumption, Distraction, and Progression countless times. A gospel-centered theology instead of a sanctification–centered or maturation–centered theology, also gives our decision-making a different focus. So for example, when we do family worship now, we don't do it because it makes us "more godly." We don't do it because it will make our children "more godly" and insure their justification and sanctification. We don't measure our sanctification by how often we do or don't do it. We do it because we love Jesus from the heart and we want our children to love Jesus. Loving Jesus protects us. Loving Jesus is what causes me to obey his commands, and knowing him is what causes me to love him. Obeying his commands will not make me love him. Loving him makes me obey. Do you see how important this logic is? When you flip the logic you're done for!

Here is a sensitive example: I struggle with disillusionment and bitterness. I have noticed that this is episodic, there are triggers and when they are set off I spiral down quickly. The days I lose this battle are the days that I verbally lash at myself for not being sanctified enough to overcome, not being "good enough," not being a lady of grace, etc. I spend my hours telling myself what a disobedient sinner I am. The days I win this battle are the days where I can stop those thoughts fairly quickly through prayers directed at Christ, I take myself to the gospel, I repeat it over and over again, I confess my sins, but I don't stop at confession—I plead before God the righteousness of Christ for myself. I appropriate the righteousness of Christ by reminding myself that when God sees me, it is not just at the "not guilty" level but as being clothed with the robes of Jesus.

We must, all our days, fight against gospel amnesia. We dare never forget the gospel.

MY HOPE FOR YOU

I end with one of my favorite ways in which Sally Lloyd-Jones describes the love of God in *The Jesus Storybook Bible*, that he loves us:

> ... with a Never Stopping, Never Giving up, Unbreaking, Always and Forever Love.

My hope in this small and humble work, is to encourage you to look at the cross, to fall in love with Jesus anew or maybe for the first time, not only for the sake of the well being of your own soul, but also in the hope that a fervent gospel-centered revival can be set ablaze "to the praise of his glorious grace."

> I know your deeds; you have the reputation of being alive, but you are dead. Wake up! (Revelation 3:1b-2a)

Further Reading

1. God Is The Gospel, John Piper
2. The Prodigal God, Timothy Keller
3. The Cross Of Christ, John Stott
4. The God Who Is There, D.A. Carson
5. Transforming Grace, Jerry Bridges
6. Surprised by Grace, Tullian Tchividjian
7. Living The Cross Centered Life, C.J. Mahaney
8. What Is The Gospel, Greg Gilbert
9. Gospel: Recovering the Power that Made Christianity Revolutionary, J.D. Greear
10. The Explicit Gospel, Matt Chandler with Jared Wilson
11. Unbelievable Gospel, Jonathan Dodson
12. The Truth Of The Cross, R.C. Sproul
13. The Jesus Storybook Bible, Sally Lloyd-Jones
14. Because He Loves Me, Elyse M. Fitzpatrick
15. Simply Jesus, N.T. Wright

Made in the USA
San Bernardino, CA
11 February 2014